AF843759

PUBLIC WORKS CONDITIONS OF CONTRACT FOR BUILDING WORKS DESIGNED BY THE EMPLOYER

EXPLAINED

SECOND EDITION

PUBLIC WORKS CONDITIONS OF CONTRACT FOR BUILDING WORKS DESIGNED BY THE EMPLOYER

EXPLAINED

SECOND EDITION

By

JAMES HOWLEY

&

MARTIN LANG

CLARUS
PRESS

Published by
Clarus Press Ltd,
Griffith Campus,
South Circular Road,
Dublin 8.
www.claruspress.ie

Typeset by
Gough Typesetting Services,
Dublin

Printed by
SprintPrint

ISBN
978-1-911611-03-5

A catalogue record for this book is available from the British Library

All rights reserved. No part of this publication may be reproduced, or transmitted in any form or by any means, including recording and photocopying, without the written permission of the copyright holder, application for which should be addressed to the publisher. Written permission should also be obtained before any part of the publication is stored in a retrieval system of any nature.

All materials reproduced with the kind permission of the Oireachtas and Department of Finance who hold copyright in the rules ©

Disclaimer
Whilst every effort has been made to ensure that the contents of this book are accurate, neither the publisher, editor or contributors can accept responsibility for any errors or omissions or loss occasioned to any person acting or refraining from acting as result of any material in this publication.

Joint Copyright © Clarus Press and Howley & Lang 2018

ABOUT THE AUTHORS

James Howley MSc, Dip Arb, Dip Proj Mgmt, MRICS, FCIOB, FCIArb., Chartered Arbitrator, Chartered Surveyor, Accredited Adjudicator, CIArb Accredited Mediator with over 30 years' experience in the construction industry. In addition to building and civil engineering contractors, James has worked with professional consultancy practices. His experience includes large-scale building and civil engineering projects, including utilities, rail, roads, oil and power generating projects in Ireland, the UK, mainland Europe and the Middle East. James holds an MSc in Construction Law and Arbitration from Kings College, London and has completed formal training in arbitration, adjudication and mediation. James is currently working in private practice as a Construction Contracts Consultant, Arbitrator, Conciliator and Adjudicator.

Martin Lang is a Member of the Chartered Institute of Arbitrators, Chartered Institute Accredited Mediator and is an Engineers Ireland Assessed Conciliator. He has been involved in the construction industry for the last 40 years. Martin began his career as an Estimator and trained as a Quantity Surveyor in Dublin. He has had an extensive career in Project and Construction Management in the United Kingdom, Spain, Portugal, the Middle East and West Africa. He joined the Construction Industry Federation in 1995 as an Executive Officer, became Head of Contracts and Dispute Resolution and is now Director of Main Contracting. He has acted as Mediator and Conciliator in over 200 construction related disputes as well as being involved in the development of national training programmes and advice services in relation to pre-tender, pre-qualification issues, contract documents, claims management dispute resolution, public sector procurement etc. He is a practicing Mediator and Conciliator.

PREFACE

The introduction of the new Public Works Contracts in 2007 brought significant change to the construction industry and influenced how construction would operate on public construction projects. The objective of the new Public Works Contracts was to secure a public procurement system that would provide certainty with regards to time for delivery of construction projects and certainty of cost. The Public Works Contracts incorporated international trends in the procurement and execution of public construction projects. Contractors had to adapt to the changes, be aware of the significant transfer of risk and the obligations for contract compliance in order to maintain entitlements.

The first edition of *Public Works Contract for Building Works Designed by the Employer: Explained* was published in 2008. Fully updated this new edition explains each contract clause in a clear and easy to understand manner to allow the reader to develop an insight into how these contracts will operate. This book also included sample documents, including notices and letters, which will add to the readers' understanding of the strict and critical administrative procedures demanded by these contracts.

Since 2008, further significant changes have been made to the Public Works Contracts. This book is based on the Public Works Contract for Building Works Designed by the Employer 28 June 2016 edition.

CONTENTS

INTRODUCTION

PUBLIC WORKS CONTRACTS

New Public Works Contracts

The new Public Works Contracts were first published on 19 February 2007. These contracts are now the norm for all public works contracts. Since the first publication of the Public Works Contracts, numerous amendments have been made to the Forms of Contract to incorporate both new legislation that affects the construction industry and submissions made to the government by construction bodies.

This book is a commentary on the current contract conditions for the *Public Works Contract For Building Works Designed By The Employer*. It is the intention of this book to explain the most significant contract clauses that affect contractors in a clear and easy to understand manner and to allow the reader to develop an insight into how these contracts operate. This book also includes sample documents, including notices and letters, which will add to the readers' understanding of the strict and critical administrative procedures demanded by these contracts.

There are 13 conditions set out using the following headings:

1. The Contract
2. The Law
3. Loss Damage and Injury (Insurances)
4. Management
5. Contractors Personnel
6. Property
7. The Site
8. Quality Testing and Defects
9. Time and Completion
10. Claims and Adjustments
11. Payment
12. Termination
13. Disputes.

Areas of particular importance are dealt with in clauses 4, 9, 10, 11 and 13. These clauses are dealt with in particular detail in the commentary sections. The contractor's recovery of costs and time have been set to contractual conditions that are "condition precedent". This means that the contract criteria must be complied with by the contractor within set time periods if the contractor is to succeed in recovery of entitlements. In line with developments in the international construction markets and other jurisdictions "time-bar" clauses are incorporated into the contract. Contractor's claims can fail, if the time-scales for the provision of initial notices of claims and the provision of full details of claims are not provided within the time-scales dictated within the contract.

HOW TO USE THIS BOOK

This book reproduces the current form of contract. The book is set out in a clause by clause basis following the same format as set out in the form of contract. The commentaries on clauses of particular interest are contained in the highlighted print, giving practical explanations on the intent of the contract.

CONDITIONS

1 THE CONTRACT

1.1 Definitions

The following terms have the following meanings in the Contract:

Term	*Meaning*
Adjudication	means adjudication under the Construction Contracts Act 2013 **Note** The Construction Contracts Act 2013 was enacted to eliminate pay when paid clauses and to ensure a default timescale for payments. The Act also incorporated rapid dispute resolution procedures which are binding in the interim and which is binding for the supply chain. A copy of the Construction Contracts Act 2013 can be found at www.irishstatutebook.ie/eli/2013/act/34/enacted/en/html
Ancillary Certificate	a certificate as prescribed by the Building Control Regulations, other than a statutory certificate of compliance, given by a competent person to confirm compliance of elements of the building, design or Works with Building Regulations; and "Ancillary Certifier" means the person proposed to issue such a certificate. **Note** A copy of the Building Control (Amendment) Regulations 2014 SI No 9 of 2014 can be found at: http://www.housing.gov.ie/sites/default/files/migrated-files/en/Legislation/DevelopmentandHousing/BuildingStandards/FileDownLoad%2C35135%2Cen.pdf
Assigned Certifier	the person so assigned by the Employer to certify compliance with the relevant requirements under the Building Control Regulations. **Note** A copy of the Building Control Regulations February 2014 Code of Practice for Inspecting and Certifying Buildings and Works Department of Environment Community and Local Government can be found at: http://www.housing.gov.ie/housing/building-standards/building-regulations/code-practice-inspecting-and-certifying-buildings
Building Control Regulations	the Building Control Regulations 1997-2014 and any amendments thereto. **Note** A copy of the Building Control (Amendment) Regulations 2014 SI No 9 of 2014 can be found at: http://www.housing.gov.ie/sites/default/files/migrated-files/en/Legislation/DevelopmentandHousing/BuildingStandards/FileDownLoad%2C35135%2Cen.pdf

Term	*Meaning*
Change Order	an instruction of the Employer's Representative to change [including add to or omit from] the Works or to change [including impose or remove] constraints in the Contract on how the Works are to be executed.
Code of Practice for Inspecting and Certifying Buildings and Works	The code of practice published by the Department of Environment, Community and Local Government with reference to Article 20G of the Building Control Regulations. **Note** A copy of the Code of Practice for Inspecting and Certifying Buildings and Works can be found at: http://www.housing.gov.ie/housing/building-standards/building-regulations/code-practice-inspecting-and-certifying-buildings
Consent	planning permission, order, approval, certificate, Ancillary Certificate, fire certificate, licence, permit, environmental impact statement, or other consent required by Legal Requirement for the execution or completion of the Works, or identified as a Consent in the Works Requirements.
Contract Date	the date the Employer issued the Letter of Acceptance.
Contract Sum	the amount identified in the Agreement as the initial Contract Sum, as adjusted in accordance with the Contract.
Contractor's Documents	drawings, specifications, manuals, reports, Consents and other [eye readable and machine readable] written material relating to the Works that the Contractor uses, prepares or gives to the Employer or any other person, or is to use, prepare or give to the Employer or any other person • under the Works Requirements or • under any Legal Requirement or • to obtain any Consent or • in connection with a proposal under sub-clause 4.8. **Note** "Contractor's Documents" means drawings, specifications, manuals, reports and other written material relating to the Works. This could be the Contractor's applications for consents under the Contract for which he may be responsible. Such responsibilities will be contained within the Contract Documents.
Contractor's Things	equipment, facilities and other things the Contractor [or Contractor's Personnel] uses on or adjacent to the Site to execute the Works, except Works Items.
Contractor's Personnel	the Contractor's representative, supervisor and Subcontractors, employees and other persons working on or adjacent to the Site for the Contractor or Subcontractors, and other persons assisting the Contractor to perform the Contract.

Term	*Meaning*
Date for Substantial Completion of the Works or a Section	the date identified as the Date for Substantial Completion of the Works or Section in the Schedule, part 1G or 2C, and, if the Schedule states a period, the last day of that period, starting on the Contract Date, in either case as adjusted in accordance with the Contract.
Defect	non-compliance of the Works or a Works Item with the Contract [including a failed test and, after Substantial Completion, work that has not been completed].
Defects Certificate	a certificate of the Employer's Representative that the Defects Period has ended.
Defects Period	the period starting on Substantial Completion of the Works and continuing for the period stated in the Schedule, as may be extended under sub-clause 8.6.2.
Designated Date	the date 10 days before the last day for receipt of the Contractor's tender for the Works, or, if there was none, 10 days before the Employer received the Contractor's tender for the Works.

Employer's Personnel any of the following:

- the Employer's Representative
- the Employer's employees, agents and consultants in connection with the Contract when acting on behalf of the Employer but not when exercising authority under Law
- other contractors of the Employer working on the Site when acting within the scope of their contracts with the Employer
- anyone else the Employer's Representative notifies the Contractor is Employer's Personnel.
- Assigned Certifier

> **Note**
> Refer to note under Building Control Regulations.
>
> Employer's Personnel can also include other contractors engaged by the Employer on the site.

Employer's Representative the architect, engineer, quantity surveyor or other person appointed by the Employer as its representative in accordance with the Contract.

Inspection Plan the document prepared by the Assigned Certifier in accordance with the Code of Practice for Inspecting and Certifying Buildings and Works having regard to the Works Requirements. The Inspection Plan also includes the Inspection Notification Framework, both of which may be amended by the Assigned Certifier from time to time.

> **Note**
> Details of the contents of the Inspection Plan prepared by the Assigned Certifier can be found at:
> http://www.housing.gov.ie/housing/building-standards/building-regulations/code-practice-inspecting-and-certifying-buildings

Term	*Meaning*
Inspection Notification Framework	the document prepared by the Assigned Certifier and agreed with the Contractor and the Employer in accordance with the Code of Practice for Inspecting and Certifying Buildings and Works identifying key stages or items of work that individual certifiers and the Assigned Certifier are to be notified by the Contractor as the Works are ready for inspection. **Note** Details of the contents of the Inspection Notification Framework can be found at: http://www.housing.gov.ie/housing/building-standards/building-regulations/code-practice-inspecting-and-certifying-buildings
Law	enactments and statutory instruments, each as defined by the Interpretation Act 2005, and regulations, directives and decisions of the European Union having direct effect in Ireland.
Legal Requirement	a requirement that applies to the Works as a result of any of the following: • Law • a Consent • a decision of an Irish court, the European Court of Justice or the European Court of First Instance • the requirements of any person having authority in connection with the Works under any Law • the requirements of any person with whose systems the Works will connect • the legal rights of any person.
Letter of Acceptance	the Employer's letter to the Contractor accepting the Contractor's tender.
Project Board	means the Project Board outlined in sub-clause 4.15.4 in the Contract
Section	a part of the Works identified as a Section in the Schedule, part 1G. **Note** The Project Board is comprised of the individuals so identified to be members in the Schedule Part 3A of the Contract.
Site	any place • where the Works are to be executed according to the Contract or • provided by the Employer for the Works or • where the Contractor is to operate or maintain Employer's facilities or that the Works Requirements identify as part of the Site.

Term	*Meaning*
Site Working Day	a day on which, according to the Contract and the Contractor's programme most recently submitted to the Employer's Representative, the Contractor is to execute the Works on the Site.

Note

Site Working Day, as opposed to "working day", is a day indicted to be a working day by the last accepted programme. It is an important definition as it is only site working days for which an extension of time can be allowed. It has a particular effect on claims occurring during a holiday period: if they are not accounted for in the programme they may be ignored in the calculation of the extension of time.

Specialist any of the following:

- a Subcontractor or supplier of a Works Item named in the Contract
- Contractor's Personnel who do or are to do design
- Contractor's Personnel stated in the Works Requirements to be Specialists.

Standing Conciliator the person appointed by the Parties, if so stated in Schedule Part 1N, and identified in Schedule Part 3C

Note

For Contract Values in excess of €10m the appointment of a Standing Conciliator is mandatory.

Where there is a Standing Conciliator, the Standing Conciliator shall be named in Schedule Part 3C and appointed prior to the Starting Date.

Starting Date the day the Contractor proposes to start executing the Works, as notified by the Contractor to the Employer's Representative under sub-clause 9.1.

Subcontractor a person to whom the execution of part of the Works is subcontracted [by the Contractor or another Subcontractor].

Term	*Meaning*
Substantial Completion of the Works or a part of the Works [including a Section]	all of the following have happened: (1) the Works or the part of the Works are complete so that they can be taken over and used by the Employer for their intended purpose and there are no Defects other than (a) Defects accepted by the Employer under sub-clause 8.5.4 or (b) minor Defects to which all of the following apply: (i) they do not prevent the Works or the part from being used for their intended purpose (ii) the Employer's Representative considers the Contractor has reasonable grounds for not promptly rectifying them (iii) rectification will not prejudice the safe and convenient use of the Works or the part (2) all tests that are required by the Contract to be passed before Substantial Completion have been passed (3) the Contractor has given the Employer's Representative the Contractor's Documents that the Contract requires be provided before Substantial Completion (4) the Contractor has given the Employer's Representative the collateral warranties that the Contract requires for the Works or part (5) the details in the Certificate of Compliance on Completion of the Works or a part thereof have been included on the Register maintained under Part IV of the Building Control Regulations. **Note** Substantial Completion includes conditions that all tests required have been completed and passed (before Substantial Completion can occur). The Contractor must provide the documents as required by the Contract to the Employer or Employer's Representative including all collateral warranties before Substantial Completion can occur. Management and production of all such documentation is essential for the Contractor.
VAT	the value-added tax payable in Ireland under Law.
Works Item	a part of the Works, anything that the Contractor intends will become part of the Works, or temporary works for the Works.

1.2. Interpretation

1.2.1 The parties intend the Contract to be given purposeful meaning for efficiency and public benefit generally and as particularly identified in the Contract.

1.2.2 Unless the context indicates otherwise, in the Contract

(1) References to the **Works** are to the works described in the Works Requirements.
(2) Words in the singular include the plural and vice versa.
(3) References to an **individual** are to a human person.
(4) References to a **person** include human persons and corporate and unincorporated bodies.
(5) Words in any gender include all genders.
(6) References to any **Law** include amendments and replacements.
(7) References to the **Contract** or any other writing include amendments.
(8) References to a **day** mean a calendar day.

(9) References to a **week** mean a period of 7 days.

(10) References to a **month** mean a calendar month.

(11) References to a **working day** mean a day that is not Saturday, Sunday, a public holiday established under the Organisation of Working Time Act 1997 or Good Friday.

(12) References to a requirement to **submit** a document or proposed course of action to Employer's Representative mean to submit it according to sub-clause 4.7, or another procedure that applies according to the Works Requirements, and sub-clause 4.7 or the Works Requirements shall apply in every such case. [Accordingly the Contractor may not implement the submission until permitted by sub-clause 4.7 or the Works Requirements.]

(13) References to the Contractor's **current programme** are to the programme in the Works Proposals, if there is one, if not, to the programme first submitted by the Contractor under sub-clause 4.9, or, in either case, to any later programme submitted by the Contractor if the period for the Employer's Representative to review it has passed and there is no outstanding objection.

(14) References to **liability** include claims, demands and proceedings.

(15) Terms such as **including**, **in particular**, **such as**, and **for example**, are not to be read as exhaustive, or to limit, but may extend, the generality of the provisions to which they relate.

(16) References to the **Agreement** and **Schedule** are to the attached agreement and completed schedule.

(17) References to the **Works Requirements**, **Works Proposals** and the **Pricing Document** are to the Works Requirements, Works Proposals and Pricing Document identified in the Schedule, part 1B; in the case of Works Requirements, as changed by Change Orders; and in the case of Works Proposals, as changed under sub-clause 4.6.2.

(18) References to **Delay Events** and **Compensation Events** are to events identified as Delay Events and Compensation Events in the Schedule, part 1K.

(19) References to the **initial** Contract Sum are to the Contract Sum stated in the Agreement; references to an initial Date for Substantial Completion are to a Date for Substantial Completion identified in the Schedule; and references to the initial Works Requirements are to the Works Requirements identified in the Schedule.

(20) The Parties are the Employer and the Contractor

1.2.3 Clarifications, examples and reminders are included occasionally in square brackets to show that no significance is to be given to their absence elsewhere.

1.2.4 No rule of legal interpretation applies to the disadvantage of a Party on the basis that the Party provided the Contract or any of it or that a term of the Contract is for the Party's benefit.

1.3 Inconsistencies

1.3.1 Except when the Contract states otherwise, the documents in the Contract are to be taken as mutually explanatory of each other if possible. If there is an inconsistency between the documents, they take precedence as follows:

- First, the Agreement, even if it has not been executed
- Second, the attached Schedule and the Letter of Acceptance and any post-tender clarifications listed in it
- Third, the Contractor's completed form of tender (excluding other documents in the tender)
- Fourth, these Conditions
- Fifth, the Works Requirements
- Sixth, the Pricing Document
- Seventh, the Works Proposals, if there are any

- Eighth, any other documents in the Contract

1.3.2 If either Party becomes aware of any inconsistency between terms of the Contract, it shall promptly inform the other Party.

1.3.3 If there is an inconsistency between figured and scaled dimensions, the figured dimensions prevail.

1.3.4 Inconsistencies between the Works Requirements and the Pricing Document shall be resolved by an instruction from the Employer's Representative under sub-clause 4.4.1(1) of the Contract.
Where inconsistencies are found to exist between the Works Requirements and the Pricing Document the Works Requirements take precedence with respect to the Works to be completed and a compensation event shall arise in accordance with the Schedule, Part 1K (17).

Note
Inconsistencies should be promptly notified. No action is identified in the Contract, however, precedence of documents applies.

As a result of Circular 01.16 January 2016, the Bill of Quantities takes precedence with respect to the Works to be completed.

1.4 Pricing Document and Works Proposals

Nothing in and no omission from the Pricing Document or Works Proposals limits the scope of the Works or the Contractor's obligations. Nothing in the Works Proposals imposes obligations on the Employer.

Note
This Sub-Clause should be read in conjunction with Article 4 of the Agreement.

1.5 Performance Bond

Before the Starting Date, unless the Schedule, part 1E, says that no bond is required, the Contractor shall give the Employer a performance bond in the form in the Works Requirements, or, if there is none, a form approved by the Employer. The performance bond shall be in the amount stated in the Schedule, part 1E, and shall be executed by the Contractor and by a surety approved by the Employer.

Note
Any performance bond is to be delivered before the start date notified by the Contractor. That will normally be within four weeks of the issue of the Letter of Acceptance. The same requirement applies to any parent company guarantee required. Bonds and guarantees are to comply with model forms contained within the Contract. A copy of the Performance Bond is contained in Model Form 1.6.

DOCUMENTS

1.6 Parent Company Guarantee

If the Schedule, part 2B, says that there is to be a parent company guarantee, the Contractor shall give the Employer such a guarantee before the Starting Date. It shall be executed by the parent company named in the Schedule, part 2B, and in the form in the Works Requirements, or, if there is none, a form approved by the Employer.

1.7 Joint Ventures

If the Contractor is a joint venture, consortium or other unincorporated grouping of two or more persons, those persons shall be jointly and severally liable to the Employer for the performance of the Contract.

1.8 Assignment

The Contractor may not assign the benefit of the Contract, or any part of it, without the Employer's consent.

1.9 Miscellaneous

1.9.1 The Contract and the documents referred to in it supersede all previous representations, arrangements, understandings and agreements between the Parties about the subject-matter of the Contract, and set out the entire agreement between the Parties about the subject-matter of the Contract. Neither Party has relied on any other written or oral representation, arrangement, understanding or agreement.

1.9.2 All the terms of the Contract are severable, and if any part is unenforceable, illegal or void, it is to that extent considered not to form part of the Contract, and the enforceability, legality and validity of the rest of the Contract will not be affected.

1.9.3 The Contract may only be changed by a document in writing signed by an authorised representative of each Party.

Note
This confirms that any changes to the Contract Documents can only be effected when made in writing by 'authorised persons'. Authorised persons is not defined. The Contractor should ensure that any such changes by authorised personnel have the authority of the Employer or the Employer's Representative.

1.9.4 The rights of a Party will not be prejudiced or restricted by any indulgence or forbearance extended to the other Party, and no waiver by a Party of any breach will waive any other breach.

1.10 Background Information

1.10.1 In this sub-clause 1.10 Background Information means any information made available on, before or after the Contract Date to the Contractor or to anyone on the Contractor's behalf by the Employer or by anyone acting on the Employer's behalf in connection with the Contractor's tender for the Contract, which information is not included in this Contract. Background Information also includes any information stated to be 'Background Information'.

1.10.2 The Contractor acknowledges and agrees as follows:

(1) The Employer has no liability whatsoever to the Contractor in contract, tort, under statute, or on any other basis whatsoever (including negligence and breach of statutory or other duty) in connection with Background Information.

(2) The Employer has not made and does not make any warranty, representation, or undertaking in connection with Background Information.

(3) The Employer has not authorised anyone to make any warranty, representation, or undertaking on the Employer's behalf in connection with Background Information.

(4) Without limiting anything in this sub-clause 1.10, the Contractor irrevocably and forever waives any liability that the Employer may have to the Contractor in connection with Background Information regardless of any of the following

circumstances, and the Contractor acknowledges that the Employer makes no warranty, representation, or undertaking in regard to those circumstances:

a) whether or not Background Information is correct
b) whether or not Background Information is complete
c) whether or not any testing, investigation, surveys, or other work to prepare Background Information was done negligently or in breach of statutory or other duties
d) whether or not those who carried out any testing, investigation, surveys, or other work to prepare Background Information were properly selected or supervised
e) whether or not Background Information was suitable for the purposes for which the Contractor or anyone fon the Contractor's behalf might use it
f) whether or not any errors or omissions in Background Information are major or numerous or both
g) whether or not Background Information represents all the information available to the Employer
h) whether or not any works described in Background Information are done as described in Background Information or at all
i) whether or not the Employer had or has other information that might render Background Information misleading
j) the manner in which Background Information was made available
k) whether or not the Contractor had adequate opportunity to carry out any testing, investigations, surveys, or other work or otherwise to verify Background Information.

(5) The Contractor has included in the Contract Sum for the risks that the Contractor has agreed to bear under this sub-clause 1.10.

Note

In connection with background information, it is critical for the Contractor to be aware of the significance of this Sub-Clause. Effectively, this Sub-Clause protects the Employer from any responsibility for information supplied, implied or withheld by the Employer at tender stage that effects the execution of the Works.

2 THE LAW

2.1 Law Governing the Contract

Irish law governs the Contract and its interpretation.

2.2 Compliance with Legal Requirements

The Contractor shall in performing the Contract comply with all Legal Requirements and ensure that the Contractor's Personnel comply with all Legal Requirements.

2.3 Consents

2.3.1 The Employer has obtained, or shall obtain, the Consents that the Works Requirements say that the Employer is to obtain. The Contractor shall obtain all other Consents.

2.3.2 The Contractor shall give and comply with all notices and pay all taxes, fees and charges required under Legal Requirements to be paid in connection with performing the Contract, unless the Works Requirements say otherwise.

2.4 Project Supervisor

2.4.1 If the Schedule, part 1C, states that the Contractor is to be appointed project supervisor for the construction stage in accordance with the Safety, Health and Welfare at Work (Construction) Regulations 2013 (the **Construction Regulations**) for the Works, or a project including the Works, the Contractor shall accept the appointment by entering into the appointment in the form in the Works Requirements. If the Schedule, part 1C, states that an individual or body corporate named in the Works Proposals is to be appointed project supervisor for the construction stage in accordance with the Construction Regulations for the Works, or a project including the Works, the Contractor shall ensure that the individual or body corporate named in the Works Proposals accepts the appointment by entering into the appointment in the form in the Works Requirements. The Contractor shall, if appointed as project supervisor, comply with its obligations under the Construction Regulations in connection with that appointment. If the Employer terminates the appointment of the Contractor or other person named in the Works Proposals as project supervisor for the construction stage as a result of that project supervisor's failure to comply with its obligations, the Contractor shall pay to the Employer all the Employer's cost resulting from the termination [including the cost of appointing and fees and expenses paid to a replacement project supervisor, or, if the Employer acts as project supervisor itself, the Employer's cost of doing so].

Note

If a Contractor takes on this role and fails to adequately perform, resource and provide the necessary insurances the Employer may terminate the Contractor's role and appoint another party to carry out the duties of project supervisor (construction stage). In this event the Contractor is replaced in this role and the Contractor is responsible for all the Employer's costs involved in the new appointment.

A copy of the Construction Regulations can be found at:
http://www.hsa.ie/eng/Legislation/New_Legislation/SI_291_2013.pdf

2.4.2 If the Contractor or a person named in the Works Proposals is to be appointed as project supervisor for the construction stage, the Contractor represents and warrants to the Employer that the Contractor or person named in the Works Proposals is competent and will allocate adequate resources to enable itself to perform its duties under the Construction Regulations.

2.4.3 If the Contractor or a person named in the Works Proposals is appointed as project supervisor for the construction stage the Contractor shall ensure that the project supervisor has the insurances required of the project supervisor under its appointment.

Note
If the Employer appoints a person other than the Contractor as Project Supervisor, the Contractor is obliged to comply with all the requirements of the Project Supervisor.

2.4.4 The Contractor shall [without adjustment to the Contract Sum or extension of time] comply with all the lawful directions of the project supervisors appointed for the construction stage and the design process in accordance with the Construction Regulations for the Works, or any project including the Works, and give them any copies of Contractor's Documents that they may request.

2.4.5 The Contractor shall, before Substantial Completion of the Works or any Section, give the Employer the documents required for the safety file (as defined in the Construction Regulations).

Note
Failure to comply with the Contract requirements for the Safety File will result in delay to the of Substantial Completion of the Works.

2.5 Safety, Health and Welfare at Work Act 2005 and Safety, Health and Welfare at Work (Construction) Regulations 2013

2.5.1 The Contractor shall [without limiting other obligations] ensure, so far as is reasonably practicable, that the Works are constructed to be safe and without risk to health, and that the Works comply in all respects, as appropriate, with the relevant statutory provisions.

2.5.2 The Contractor represents and warrants to the Employer that the Contractor is, and will, while performing the Contract, be a competent person for the purpose of ensuring, so far as is reasonably practicable, that the Works are constructed to be safe and without risk to health and that they comply in all respects, as appropriate, with the relevant statutory provisions.

2.5.3 The Contractor represents and warrants to the Employer that the Contractor is and will, while performing the Contract, be a competent person to carry out the Works and has allocated and will allocate sufficient resources to enable itself to comply with the requirements and prohibitions imposed on the Contractor by or under the relevant statutory provisions.

2.5.4 In this sub-clause 2.5 and sub-clause 2.4, **competent person**, **reasonably practicable** and **relevant statutory provisions** are construed according to section 2 of the Safety, Health and Welfare at Work Act 2005.

2.6 Ethics in Public Office

The Contractor warrants that

2.6.1 neither the Contractor nor any person on the Contractor's behalf has offered, given or agreed to give to the Employer or to any of the Employer's Personnel any gift or consideration of any kind in connection with the Contract, nor will they make such an offer, gift or agreement and

2.6.2 neither the Contractor nor any person on the Contractor's behalf has committed any offence under the Prevention of Corruption Acts 1889 to 2010 or the Ethics in Public Office Acts 1995 and 2001 in connection with the Contract, nor will they commit any such offence and

2.6.3 no Minister of the Government or Minister of State, or officer or employee of the Employer, will have or receive any share or part of the Contract or any benefit from the Contract and

2.6.4 unless fully disclosed to and agreed by the Employer in advance

(1) no former officer nor employee of the Employer nor of a consultant to the Employer whose duties related to the Works will, for 12 months after leaving the employment or office, be engaged as Contractor's Personnel and

(2) no consultant or former consultant to the Employer whose duties related to the Works will be engaged as Contractor's Personnel, except for a Specialist whose contract is to be novated from the Employer to the Contractor.

Note
This sub-clause deals with ethics in public office which contain restrictions as to the employment of personnel, including consultants, who were formerly engaged on the Works by the Employer. The sub-clause contains a prohibition on their working for the Contractor.

2.7 Legal Opinion

2.7.1 If the Contractor or any person executing a bond, guarantee, warranty or other deed or agreement required by the Contract is not an individual or a company incorporated in Ireland the Contractor shall give the Employer, together with the Agreement or other document, a legal opinion that

(1) the Contractor, or other counterparty, is an entity duly incorporated under the laws of its place of incorporation and is a separate legal entity, capable of being sued in its own name, is validly existing under the laws of that place and no steps have been taken or are being taken to appoint a receiver, examiner, administrator, liquidator, trustee or similar person over it or to wind it up and

(2) the Contractor has the necessary power and authority, and all necessary corporate and other action has been taken, to give it the power to execute, deliver and perform the obligations undertaken by it under the Contract or other document and

(3) the Contract, or other document, has been duly executed by the Contractor, or other counterparty, or on its behalf, and is binding on it under the laws of the place where it is incorporated and

(4) a judgment of an Irish court will be enforceable against the Contractor, or other counterparty, in the place where it is incorporated.

2.7.2 The opinion shall be written by a lawyer, approved by the Employer, who is authorised to practice in the place where the counterparty is incorporated. The opinion shall be in a form approved by the Employer. It shall be addressed to the Employer.

General Note on Clause 2
This section sets out the Contractor's legal obligation to carry out the Contract in accordance with the law, including legal requirements and consents obtained and required in connection with the Works Requirements.

This section, for the first time in Irish standard forms of construction contracts, introduces the requirements in relation to health, safety and welfare legislation. It is under this section that the risk of changes in legislation is passed to the Contractor.

Risks of consents are transferred to the Contractor. The Contractor shall be informed of the consents for which the Employer will be responsible. All other consents will be the responsibility of the Contractor including costs both of obtaining the consents themselves and any delay incurred while awaiting the consents.

3 LOSS, DAMAGE AND INJURY

3.1 Employer's Risks of Loss and Damage to the Works

The Employer shall bear the risk of loss of or damage to the Works resulting from any of the following:

(1) war, invasion, act of foreign enemies, hostilities whether war is declared or not, civil war, rebellion, revolution, insurrection, military or usurped power

(2) pressure waves caused by aircraft or other airborne objects travelling at sonic or supersonic speeds

(3) contamination by radioactivity or radioactive, toxic, explosive or other hazardous properties of any explosive nuclear assembly or its components, in each case not caused by the Contractor or the Contractor's Personnel

(4) terrorism, but only if terrorism is a permitted exclusion from the Contractor's insurance of the Works

(5) use or occupation of the Works by the Employer or the Employer's Personnel, other than

(a) as provided for in the Contract or

(b) to the extent that the loss or damage is caused by the negligence of the Contractor or the Contractor's Personnel, or the Contractor's breach of the Contract (subject to sub-clause 3.8 if it applies)

(6) design of the Works by the Employer or Employer's Personnel, but not if the design is covered by insurance required under the Contract.

3.2 Care of the Works

3.2.1 The Contractor shall have full responsibility for the care of, and risk of loss of and damage to, the Works, Works Items, Contractor's Things, Works Requirements, Works Proposals, Contractor's Documents, and anything the Employer gives the Contractor for the Works (together, **Risk Items**) from and including the Starting Date until and including the date the Employer's Representative issues the certificate of Substantial Completion of the Works (or in respect of a Section, the date the Employer's Representative issues the certificate of Substantial Completion of the Section, or in respect of a part of the Works that the Employer takes over under sub-clause 9.7, the date the Employer takes over the part). After that date, the Contractor shall be responsible for loss of and damage to Risk Items due to any of the following:

(1) Defects

(2) occurrences before the Employer's Representative issued the certificate of Substantial Completion (or, where applicable, before the Employer took over the part)

(3) activities of the Contractor or Contractor's Personnel.

But the Contractor's responsibility under this sub-clause 3.2 excludes loss of and damage to the Works that is at the Employer's risk under sub-clause 3.1.

3.2.2 The Contractor shall promptly rectify any loss and damage to Risk Items for which it is responsible under this sub-clause 3.2 [at its own expense if there are not sufficient insurance proceeds].

3.2.3 If loss of or damage to the Works, for which the Contractor is not responsible under this sub-clause 3.2, occurs before the Defects Certificate is issued, the Contractor shall rectify it in accordance with any instruction of the Employer.

3.3 Insurance of the Works and Other Risk Items

3.3.1 From the Starting Date, the Contractor shall insure the Works and other Risk Items against loss and damage. The insurance shall name the Contractor, the Employer and any other persons the Employer requires as insured. The insurance shall be kept in place for each Section until the date that the certificate of Substantial Completion of the Section is issued, and for the Works, except Sections that have a certificate of Substantial Completion, until the date that the certificate of Substantial Completion of the Works is issued. If so required in the Schedule, part 1D, the insurance for any Section or part of the Works that has reached Substantial Completion shall be extended until the Employer's Representative certifies Substantial Completion of the whole of the Works. In any event, after Substantial Completion, the insurance shall be kept in place until the Defects Certificate is issued, to cover loss and damage for which the Contractor remains responsible under the Contract. The limit of the insurance shall be, except for loss of or damage to Contractor's Things and Employer's property, for the full reinstatement cost of the property insured, including the cost of demolition, removal of debris, delivery, professional fees, inflation occurring during the construction and reinstatement periods, and profit. The sum insured for professional fees shall include at least the percentage of the Contract Sum stated in the Schedule, part 1D. The insurance shall include any Employer's property listed in the Schedule, part 1D, and the indemnity limit for those items shall be as stated in the Schedule.

3.3.2 The proceeds of the insurance of the Works, less the portion to cover professional fees that the Employer is to pay, shall be paid into a bank account in the joint names of the Employer and the Contractor. They shall be paid out of the account to the Contractor in instalments on the basis of interim payment certificates of the Employer's Representative of the Contract value of the work done and Works Items delivered to the Site to rectify the loss or damage, following generally sub-clause 11.1, and also paid out of the account to the Employer for its other costs. Any balance remaining in the account after the work of rectification is complete shall be paid to the Employer.

3.4 Contractor's Indemnity

3.4.1 The Contractor shall indemnify the Employer and the Employer's employees against

(1) liability and

(2) loss of and damage to the Employer's property [including the Site], unless excluded under sub-clause 3.8

arising from or in the course of the Contractor's performance or non-performance of the Contract.

3.4.2 The Contractor's indemnity in this sub-clause 3.4 does not apply to the Employer's liability under the Contract to the Contractor; nor does it apply to liability to the extent that the liability is covered by the Employer's indemnities in sub-clauses 3.5 and 6.2.

3.5 Employer's Indemnity

The Employer shall indemnify the Contractor against:

(1) liability for death, injury, or illness of any person or loss of or damage to any physical property that the Contractor incurs in the course of performing the Contract to the extent caused by the negligence of the Employer and

(2) liability for property damage that is the unavoidable result of executing the Works in accordance with the Works Requirements

3.6 Public Liability and Employer's Liability Insurances

3.6.1 From the Starting Date until the date the Defects Certificate is issued, the Contractor shall insure the Employer and the Contractor against their respective liabilities for

(1) death, injury or illness of any person and

(2) loss of or damage to any physical property and

(3) obstruction, loss of amenities, nuisance, trespass, stoppage of traffic and infringement of light, easement or quasi-easement

resulting from an accident arising from or in the course of the performance or non-performance of the Contract except to the extent covered by the Employer's indemnities in sub-clause 3.5 or sub-clause 6.2.2(2).

3.6.2 From the Starting Date until the date the Defects Certificate is issued, the Contractor shall insure itself against liability for death, injury or illness of Contractor's Personnel. For employees of Subcontractors, this obligation may be satisfied by ensuring that the Subcontractor maintains the insurance. The Contractor shall ensure that this insurance includes a provision that indemnifies the Employer against any liability for which the Contractor would be entitled to an indemnity, including costs, charges and expenses.

3.6.3 The minimum indemnity limit of the Contractor's public liability and employer's liability insurances shall be as stated in the Schedule, part 1D.

3.6.4 If the Contractor or the Contractor's Personnel return to the Site in connection with the Works after the Defects Certificate is issued, the Contractor shall ensure the insurances required by this sub-clause 3.6 are in place at all times that the Contractor or Contractor's Personnel are on Site.

3.7 Professional Indemnity Insurance

If the Schedule states that professional indemnity insurance is required, from the Starting Date until the sixth anniversary of the date that the Employer's Representative certifies Substantial Completion of the Works, or any other period stated in the Schedule, part 1D, the Contractor shall maintain professional indemnity insurance for its performance of the Contract. The indemnity limit shall be at least that stated in the Schedule, part 1D. This insurance shall include retroactive cover to when the Contractor's design of the Works and Works Items started.

3.8 Existing Facilities and Use or Occupation by Employer

This sub-clause 3.8 shall apply only if so stated in the Schedule, part 1D.

To the extent that (a) the Works involve alteration or extension of existing facilities owned by the Employer, or (b) the Employer uses or occupies the Works, the Employer shall bear the risk of loss of or damage to those facilities and the part of the Works used or occupied by the Employer, and their contents owned by the Employer, caused by any of the following perils, as defined in the Works Requirements or, if not defined there, in standard fire and specified perils insurance policies available in Ireland:

(1) fire, storm, tempest, flood
(2) bursting or overflowing of water tanks, apparatus or pipes
(3) explosion, impact, aircraft
(4) riot, civil commotion or malicious damage.

but the Contractor shall bear the risk of such loss and damage to the extent caused by the negligence of the Contractor or Contractors Personnel to the extent (and up to the limit) required to be insured under sub-clause 3.6.1.

3.9 General Requirements Concerning Insurance

3.9.1 The insurance required by the Contract (the **Insurance**) shall be placed with reputable insurers approved by the Employer.

3.9.2 The only exclusions from the Insurance shall be those listed in the Schedule, part 1D. The levels of excess shall be no higher than stated in the Schedule, part 1D.

3.9.3 The Insurance shall include any extensions and comply with any additional requirements in the Schedule and the Works Requirements.

3.9.4 Liability Insurance on which the Employer is required to be insured shall include a cross-liability clause. All Insurance on which the Employer is required to be insured shall provide that the insurer accepts the term "insured" as applying to each insured person as if a separate policy of insurance had been issued to each of them, but without the overall limit of indemnity being increased as a result, and that non-compliance by the Contractor or any other insured will not affect the Employer's rights.

3.9.5 The Contractor shall comply with the terms of the Insurance policies.

3.9.6 Within 10 working days of being requested to do so, the Contractor shall give the Employer evidence to the Employer's satisfaction that the Insurances are in effect, including copies of policies and receipts for premiums. For professional indemnity insurance, a certificate in the form included in the Works Requirements, or, if there is none, a form approved by the Employer, signed by the broker or underwriter, may be given instead of a copy of the professional indemnity policy.

3.9.7 The Contractor shall not make any material reduction to the Insurance cover unless approved in advance by the Employer. The Contractor shall promptly notify the Employer of any cancellation, renewal, non-renewal or material reduction by the insurer of any Insurance policy.

3.9.8 If the Contractor fails to maintain any of the Insurances in the terms required by the Contract, the Employer shall be entitled [without affecting its other rights] to take out the insurance and pay the premiums, and the Contractor shall pay the amount of the premiums to the Employer on demand.

3.9.9 If the Works Requirements include provision for an owner controlled insurance programme, the Parties shall comply with those provisions, including any amendments they make to this clause 3.

General Note on Clause 3

This section of the Contract sets out the risks that each party will bear in respect of loss or damage to the Works and includes the insurance requirements and the Contractor's obligation to take care of the Works both during the life of the project and after Practical Completion until the Defects Certificate is issued by the Employer's Representative.

The indemnities to be provided by the Contractor and the Employer are detailed, including the fact that the Employer may require professional indemnity cover for any element of design to be carried out by the Contractor his personnel.

The definition of "liability" under this Contract is broad. It is possible that the indemnity provisions may extend to a Contractor's liability to consequential and indirect losses incurred. Contractors should seek advice from their brokers or insurance agents on these provisions.

The Contractor must have the required insurances in place before the start date. Evidence of this has to be produced within 10 working days of a request from the Employer, including copies of policies and receipts for premiums paid. From a contract-administration point of view, no change in insurance levels is allowed without advance notice and approval from the Employer. The Employer, on default, can take out his own insurance and recover the cost from the Contractor. The Employer may require the Contractor to extend his All Risks insurance to cover the Employer's own facilities and contents for standard perils. Contractor's should note that terrorism and asbestos indemnities may be listed as possible exclusions.

4 MANAGEMENT

4.1 Co-operation

4.1.1 The Employer [subject to restraints as a public authority] and the Contractor shall support reciprocal co-operation for the Contract purposes, including co-operation with and between Contractor's Personnel and Employer's Personnel.

4.1.2 Such support may be relevant particularly to any of the following:

(1) negotiation of agreements provided for in the Contract
(2) value engineering
(3) use of most effective and compatible electronic and other methods of communicating and recording
(4) efficient order and timing of information provided for in the Contract
(5) minimising the effects of suspension
(6) Efforts by the Contractor to minimise delay and Compensation Events and their effects
(7) Contractor's flexible management

4.1.3 Either Party, or the Employer's Representative, may request clarifications, consultations, workshops, exchange of information and expertise, or investigations, although not provided for elsewhere in the Contract. The request shall specify purposes and, as relevant, proposed participants, arrangements, methods and any proposals for recording or agreeing results.

4.1.4 The Parties may agree to consult or communicate, without prejudice. In any case, offering or giving co-operation does not imply any admission of any responsibility or alter either Party's rights or duties unless otherwise agreed in writing. The Parties shall convene meetings of the Project Board to review, without prejudice, disputes referred thereto.

Note

In addition to the Contractor's entitlements under Sub-Clause 4.1.3, the Parties may decide, where appropriate, to involve the Project Board in an unprejudiced procedure to attempt to resolve any disputes that may arise during the course of the Works. The usefulness of the co-operation sub-clause may assist in the resolution of disputes without recourse to the formal dispute resolution procedures.

This sub-clause provides a useful facility to have all matters or any contentious matters examined to determine the basis of any instruction or decision of the Employer's Representative and to examine whether the Contractor has any entitlements arising from the determination of the Employer's Representative.

4.2 Contractor's Representative and Supervisor

4.2.1 The Contractor shall appoint, before the Starting Date

(1) a representative with full authority to act on behalf of the Contractor in all matters concerning the Contract and
(2) a full-time supervisor of all the Contractor's activities on the Site, with full authority to receive instructions and other communications on behalf of the Contractor in all matters concerning the Contract.

The representative and the supervisor may, but need not, be the same person.

4.2.2 Matters of which the Contractor's representative or supervisor are aware [including communications and instructions] are presumed to be within the Contractor's knowledge.

4.2.3 If the Contractor's representative or supervisor are named in the Works Proposals, the Contractor shall appoint the individuals named. If not, or either of them is changed, the Contractor shall submit details of the proposed representative or supervisor to the Employer's

Representative. If the Contractor's representative or supervisor dies, or becomes incapable of performing their role, or is no longer available to the Contractor, the Contractor shall appoint a suitable replacement, having submitted details to the Employer's Representative. If the Employer's Representative so requires because of the misconduct, negligence or incompetence of either of them, the Contractor shall remove its representative or supervisor and appoint a suitable replacement, having submitted details to the Employer's Representative.

Note
This sub-clause deals with the Contractor's supervision. The Contractor must notify the Employer's Representative of the name of the Contractor's representative or supervisor before the start date. If named in the Work Proposals, they shall be the persons appointed unless a change is notified to the Employer's Representative. The Employer's Representative has the power to have the Contractor remove a Contractor's representative or supervisor arising from misconduct, negligence or incompetence. The Contractor shall comply with the Employer's Representative's requirement having submitted details to the Employer's Representative.

4.3 Employer's Representative

4.3.1 If the Employer's Representative is not named in the Schedule, part 1A, the Employer shall, promptly after the Contract Date, appoint, and notify the Contractor of the identity of, the Employer's Representative.

4.3.2 If there are limitations on the authority of the Employer's Representative to perform its functions or powers under the Contract, they are stated in the Contract. But any act or instruction of the Employer's Representative under the Contract shall have effect as if within the Employer's Representative's authority, and the Contractor need not inquire into whether the Employer has actually authorised it.

4.3.3 The Employer's Representative may delegate in writing to named representatives any functions or powers under the Contract and revoke any delegation. The appointment of such a representative shall not prevent the Employer's Representative from exercising directly any functions or powers. The Employer's Representative shall notify the Contractor and the Employer of any delegation, and the names of representatives, and of any subsequent changes, within 5 working days after the event in each case.

4.3.4 Any opinion, certificate, determination, assessment or objection of the Employer's Representative under the Contract may be revised in accordance with clause 13, except for decisions stated in the Contract to be conclusive [such as rejection of a value engineering proposal under sub-clause 4.8 or rejection of a Defect under sub-clause 8.5.4].

4.3.5 The Employer may replace the Employer's Representative at any time, notifying the Contractor of the replacement, and shall do so promptly if the position of Employer's Representative becomes vacant before the Defects Certificate (or alternatively the certificates required following termination) have been issued. Pending appointment of a replacement, the Employer shall carry out the functions and powers of the Employer's Representative.

4.4 Employer's Representative's Communications

4.4.1 The Employer's Representative may give the Contractor
(1) instructions, which are either
(a) directions in accordance with the Contract or
(b) Change Orders and
(2) objections, in accordance with sub-clause 4.7

4.4.2 The Employer's Representative may give the Contractor or the Employer, or both

(1) opinions, assessments, determinations and certificates, in accordance with the Contract and

(2) other communications [including clarifications] in accordance with the Contract or the Employer's Representative considers appropriate.

Note

The Employer's Representative may give the Contractor instructions which can be either:

(i) Directions in accordance with the Contract; or
(ii) Change Orders.

The Employer's Representative may also object to any of the Contractor's proposals in accordance with sub-clause 4.7.

The Employer's Representative may also give opinions, assessments, determinations and certificates in accordance with the Contract and other communications, including clarifications, or as the Employer's Representative considers appropriate.

Despite the apparent restrictions mentioned under the Schedule in Part 1A, the Employer's Representative has similar powers to both the engineer and architect under the Engineers Ireland or Government Departments and Local Authorities forms. The Employer's Representative may issue instructions up to the issue of the Defects Certificate. The Employer's Representative may change the Work Requirements, impose, change or remove restrictions on the way the work is done and/or give instructions on defects.

Instructions are to be given to the Contractor when requested in the time required under sub-clause 4.10

4.5 Instructions

4.5.1 The Employer's Representative may issue instructions to the Contractor on any matter connected with the Works [whether or not mentioned elsewhere in the Contract] at any time up to the date the Defects Certificate is issued. The Contractor shall comply with an instruction of the Employer's Representative.

4.5.2 If the Employer's Representative gives an instruction and calls it a direction, but the Contractor considers that it is a Change Order, the Contractor shall be entitled to give notice under sub-clause 10.3, and have the issue determined under clause 10. In addition to the requirements of sub-clause 10.3, the Contractor must give this notice before starting to implement the instruction, otherwise it will be taken to be a direction.

4.5.3 The Employer's Representative shall not give a Change Order concerning the Works or a Section after its Substantial Completion has been certified, except concerning Defects or work to be done after Substantial Completion.

4.5.4 The Employer's Representative shall give an instruction that is, in the Employer's Representative's opinion, necessary for the completion of the Works. If, in the Employer's Representative's opinion, it is physically impossible or contrary to Legal Requirements to complete the Works in accordance with the Works Requirements, the Employer's Representative shall give a Change Order. The Employer's Representative shall give an instruction required under this sub-clause 4.5.4 within the time required by sub-clause 4.11.

4.5.5 Instructions of the Employer's Representative shall be given in writing except when there is imminent danger to safety or health or of damage to property, in which case the Employer's Representative may give oral instructions, and shall confirm them in writing as soon as practicable.

Note

The Employer's Representative issue all instructions on any matter connected with the Works at any time up to the date the Defects Certificate is issued. The Contractor must comply with all instructions. There is no facility for the Contractor to confirm or to work on verbal instructions unless on matters of health and safety.

Sub-clause 4.5.2 provides that if the Employer's Representative issues a direction which the Contractor considers to be a Change Order then the Contractor can give notice under clause 10.3 and have the matter determined under clause 10. The Contractor must give this notice before starting to implement the instruction, otherwise it will be taken to be a 'Direction'. The Employer's Representative will make a determination under sub-clause 10.5. The Contractor, if dissatisfied with the Employer's Representative's determination, can refer the matter to conciliation.

All directions should be reviewed to establish if it is a Change Order. In the event of a Change Order being issued then it is a Delay and Compensation Event under Item 1 of Section K of the Schedule, Part 1.

4.6 Works Proposals

4.6.1 The Contractor shall ensure that all Works Proposals comply with the Works Requirements.

4.6.2 If any Works Proposals do not comply with the Contract or the Works Requirements or Legal Requirements or are physically impossible to comply with, the Contractor shall propose a change to the Works Proposals as necessary. [There shall be no extension of time or adjustment to the Contract Sum for this.] If the Works Proposals need to be changed because of a change to the Works Requirements, the Contractor shall propose a change. The Contractor shall submit any change to the Works Proposals to the Employer's Representative.

Note

If any Works Proposals do not comply with the Contract or the initial Works Requirements or are physically impossible to comply with, the Contractor shall propose a change to the Works Proposals as necessary. There shall be no extension of time or adjustment to the Contract Sum for this.

Condition 4.6.2 states that:

> "If the Works Proposals need to be changed because of a change to the Works Requirements, the Contractor shall propose a change. The Contractor shall submit any change to the Works Proposals to the Employer's Representative."

This proposal comes under Item 1 of Section K of the Schedule and is a Delay Event and a Compensation Event.

Condition 4.6.1 requires the Contractor to provide a statement of the proposed action and all supporting information to the Employer's Representative.

4.7 Required Contractor Submissions

Unless the Works Requirements say that a different procedure is to apply, whenever the Contract requires that a document or proposed course of action be submitted to the Employer's Representative, the following shall apply:

4.7.1 The Contractor shall give the document or a statement of the proposed action and all necessary supporting information to the Employer's Representative.

4.7.2 The Employer's Representative may [but is not bound to] make a written objection to a Contractor's submission, giving reasons.

4.7.3 The Employer's Representative may request additional information.

4.7.4 The Employer's Representative's period for objection is 10 working days from when the Employer's Representative has received from the Contractor enough information to make a purposeful review of the matter submitted should it wish to make one.

4.7.5 The Contractor shall apply in writing for any reduction of the period that it considers desirable in the interests of the Works, which the Employer's Representative may agree if it thinks fit.

4.7.6 The Employer's Representative may alter or withdraw an objection.

4.7.7 The Contractor shall not implement any submission before the period has ended, or contrary to any outstanding objection given within the period.

4.7.8 The Contractor shall make a new submission to meet any objection given within the period.

4.7.9 The Contractor shall also make new submissions as necessary to perform its duties under the Contract [whether or not it has received any objection], and in particular so that its submitted programme shows actual and current planned progress.

4.7.10 The Employer's Representative may object on the grounds that to proceed according to the submission
(1) would not comply with the Contract or
(2) would have an adverse effect on the Employer or the public interest or
(3) would impose an obligation on the Employer that the Contract does not require the Employer to bear or
(4) would be contrary to a Legal Requirement or
(5) would have an adverse effect on the Contractor's ability to comply with the Contract
or any other ground stated in the Contract.

4.7.11 Neither the Employer's Representative's rights to object, nor objections or their absence, reduce any of the Employer's Representative's other powers, or reduce any of the Contractor's responsibilities.

Note
The Contract may require the Contractor to provide a document(s) or a proposed course of action to the Employer's Representative. If required, the Contractor shall provide a statement of the proposed action and all supporting information to the Employer's Representative. The Employer's Representative may object to the submission giving reasons. The Employer's Representative may request additional information. The Employer's Representative has 10 working days from when Contractor has provided *enough* information to object to the submission. How the words "enough information" are satisfied is a matter for the Employer's Representative. The Contractor can request a reduction in the time for review and the Employer's Representative may or may not agree as he thinks fit. New submissions may be necessary from the Contractor and the Contractor is obliged to produce these documents. In planning the programme such time periods must be allowed by the Contractor for such approvals and the timing for submissions and approvals needs to be identified clearly on the current programme.

4.8 Value Engineering

4.8.1 The Contractor may give to the Employer's Representative a written value engineering proposal that will, if adopted, either
(1) reduce the Contract Sum or
(2) accelerate the execution of the Works, or otherwise be of benefit to the Employer, with no increase to the Contract Sum.

4.8.2 The Contractor's proposal shall include all of the following:

(1) any proposed changes to the Contract
(2) any proposed changes to the Contractor's Documents [including other Consents]
(3) a detailed breakdown of the Contractor's original tender cost for the relevant work and the projected cost of the proposal and any proposed adjustment to the Contract Sum to reflect a share of any saving
(4) details of any proposed changes to the programme.

4.8.3 The Employer's Representative shall, as soon as practicable, notify the Contractor whether the Employer agrees to or rejects the proposal. If the Employer agrees to the proposal, the Employer's Representative shall, if agreed, determine a reduction to the Contract Sum or an adjustment to the Date for Substantial Completion of the Works and any affected Section (or both) in accordance with the agreed proposal and the Contractor shall implement the agreed proposal. If the proposal is rejected, this shall be conclusive.

4.8.4 If the proposal includes a change in the design of the Works, unless otherwise agreed, the Contractor shall undertake and be liable to the Employer for that design and any other Consents.

Note
If the Contractor proposes any value engineering in order to reduce the Contract Sum or accelerate the programme the proposal must provide details of:

(i) The proposed changes to the Contract;
(ii) Proposed changes to the Contractor's Documents;
(iii) A detailed breakdown of the Contractor's original tender cost for the relevant work and the projected cost of the proposal and any proposed adjustment to the Contract Sum to reflect the saving; and
(iv) Details of the proposed changes to the programme.

A submission of this sort will require a great deal of administration. If a Contractor wishes to accelerate the programme he should have all subcontractors and suppliers in full agreement, otherwise subcontractors and suppliers would be committed to a programme that was superseded without their agreement.

If the Employer agrees to the Contractor's value engineering proposal, the saving to the Contract Sum will be determined by the Employer's Representative.

If there is a design element in the proposal then the Contractor is responsible for the design and the cost.

If a Contractor's value engineering proposal is rejected, such rejection is conclusive.

The Contractor should take into account any possible Consents (refer to definitions) that may be required as a result of its proposal as responsibility for such Consents will rest with the Contractor.

4.9 Programme

4.9.1 Before the Starting Date, the Contractor shall submit to the Employer's Representative and the Project Board members, [and the Standing Conciliator where appointed], a detailed programme having regard to the requirements of the Inspection Plan and Inspection Notification Framework. If there is a programme in the Works Proposals that complies with the Contract, the Contractor shall submit that programme, with any required additional information [such as the actual programmed dates and any Inspection Plan requirements]. The programme shall be of a quality that will permit effective monitoring of the Works and shall, except to the extent that the Works Requirements say or the Employer's Representative agrees that anything may be omitted, include details of all of the following:

(1) when the Contractor will require any instructions, Works Items or other things to

be given by the Employer, or anything else the Contract requires the Employer, the Employer's Representative or others to give the Contractor

(2) the order in which and times at which the Contractor proposes to execute the Works, including details of procurement, manufacture, delivery, installation, construction, testing, commissioning and trial operation of Works Items and the sequencing and timing of inspections and of tests

(3) when Contractor's Documents will be submitted to the Employer's Representative

(4) the Contractor's estimate of each category of Contractor's Personnel and Contractor's Things expected to be on Site for each period

(5) work to be carried out at the Site by Employer's Personnel and others as provided in the Works Requirements

(6) current critical path, critical resources, floats and other flexibility

(7) details of last review made of programme logic and durations, and of the purposes of any changes

(8) anything else required by the Works Requirements.

4.9.2 The Contractor's programme shall allow reasonable periods of time for the Employer and the Employer's Personnel to comply with their obligations under the Contract.

4.9.3 If the Contractor's programme most recently submitted to the Employer's Representative and the Project Board members, [and the Standing Conciliator where appointed], does not correspond with actual or reasonably projected progress or the Contractor's obligations, the Contractor shall, if so directed by the Employer's Representative, submit to the Employer's Representative and the Project Board members, [and the Standing Conciliator where appointed], a revised programme that complies with this sub-clause and the other provisions of the Contract, showing actual progress and progress projected by the Contractor. If the Contractor asserts that it is not possible to reach Substantial Completion of the Works or a Section by its Date for Substantial Completion, the revised programme shall show Substantial Completion by the earliest possible date. [Neither the programme nor its review will limit the Contractor's responsibility or liability for the delay.] If the Contractor fails to submit the revised programme within 15 working days of a request from the Employer's Representative, the Employer shall be entitled to withhold from the Contractor 15% of any payment to be made to the Contractor until the revised programme is submitted.

Note

The programme will be a key document under this Contract. Simple bar charts are unlikely to satisfy the new Contract requirements. An agreed computer software may very well be necessary as critical paths, critical resources, floats, flexibility, resources, procurement, commissioning details are now required to be incorporated into the programme. The programme will be a fundamental monitoring tool of the progress of the Works. The programme will be the primary document for the assessment of entitlements arising from Delay and Compensation Events.

Contractors should note that if the Contractor fails to provide a revised programme within 15 working days of a request from the Employer's Representative, then the Employer may withhold 15 percent of the value of any payment due to the Contractor until the new programme is provided.

4.10 Progress Reports

4.10.1 The Contractor shall give the Employer's Representative and the Project Board members, [and the Standing Conciliator where appointed], monthly progress reports from the Starting Date until the Contractor has completed all work outstanding on Substantial Completion of the Works. The first report shall cover the period from the Starting Date up to the end of the month in which it occurs, and each subsequent report shall cover one month. The Contractor shall give each progress report within 7 days after the end of the month it relates to. Each progress report shall be in a form agreed by the Employer's Representative.

4.10.2 Each progress report shall include all of the following, except to the extent that the Works Requirements say or the Employer's Representative agrees that any of the following may be omitted:

(1) a detailed description of progress of each stage of the Works against the Contractor's current programme
(2) the names of Specialists and the off-site suppliers of the main Works Items, and progress and location of the design, manufacture, fabrication, delivery, installation, testing and commissioning of Works Items
(3) details of the Contractor's Personnel and Contractor's Things on the Site
(4) Status of preparation and review of Contractor's Documents
(5) copies of quality assurance documents and test results and certificates
(6) details of when any instructions to be given by the Employer's Representative will be required, and any that are outstanding
(7) details of when any Works Items or other things to be given by the Employer will be required, and any that are outstanding
(8) details of any Delay Events and Compensation Events that have occurred during the period, or are unresolved, including any disputes referred to the Project Board or to conciliation or to Adjudication or to arbitration
(9) details of any accidents, injuries, hazardous incidents, environmental incidents, labour relations problems and public relations problems concerning or affecting the Works
(10) details of anything that might have an adverse effect on the execution of the Works, the steps the Contractor is taking or proposes to take to reduce those risks, and any steps that the Contractor proposes that the Employer or the Employer's Personnel take to reduce those risks
(11) anything else that the Contractor considers relevant to a progress report
(12) anything else relevant to a progress report that the Employer's Representative directs.

Note
Progress reports are, like the programme, elevated to Contract condition status. Within seven days after the end of each month the Contractor shall provide a progress report which shall include the details as outlined above.

4.11 Notice and Time for Employer's Obligations

4.11.1 The Contractor shall give the Employer's Representative at least 10 working days advance notice of the date by which the Contractor requires any instructions that the Employer's Representative is to give, or Works Items or other things that the Employer is to give, including any requirements arising from the Inspection Plan and Inspection Notification Framework.

4.11.2 The latest date for the Employer's Representative to give required instructions, or the Employer to give the Contractor any required Works Item or other thing, shall be the latest of the following:

(1) the date stated in the Contract, if any
(2) the date shown in the Contractor's current programme
(3) the date for which the Contractor first notifies the Employer's Representative under this sub-clause that it is required
(4) the date the Contractor requires the instruction, Works Item or other thing in accordance with its actual progress.

Note
The Contractor must provide 10 days advance notice of the date by which instructions are required from the Employer's Representative for work items or other things that the Employer is to provide.

This information can be developed when producing the programme. A separate letter with a request for information should also be sent to the Employer's Representative. Any failure by the Employer's Representative to provide the requested information on time may entitle the Contractor to an extension of time and costs in accordance with Item 7 of Section K of Part 1 of the Schedule.

4.12. Documents

4.12.1 The Contractor shall keep on the Site all of the following:

(1) a full up-to-date set of the Contract documents (but the Pricing Document may be unpriced), instructions of the Employer's Representative, and Contractor's Documents

(2) a log of all instructions and Contractor's Documents showing dates of issue for each and any subsequent revisions

(3) if requested by the Employer's Representative, all publications named in the Contract and the Contractor's Documents.

(4) wage records [including time sheets and copies of all pay slips] applicable to all workers [as defined in sub-clause 5.3.1].

The Employer's Representative, and any person authorised by the Employer's Representative, shall have a right of access to these at all reasonable times.

4.12.2 The Contractor shall retain the Contractor's Documents in relation to the Works for a period of six [6] years from the date of completion of the Works or if applicable from the date of termination of the Contract for any reason.

Note

The Contractor is obliged to keep a copy of all documents including documents referred to in the Contract with the exception of the Contractor's prices. All documents can be accessed by the Employer's Representative or any person authorised by the Employer's Representative.

The Contractor is obliged to retain the Contractor's Documents for a period of 6 years.

4.13 Contractor's Management

4.13.1 The Contractor's business includes expertise and experience in construction management.

4.13.2 The Works Proposals include details of the Contractor's initial management arrangements for performing its Contract responsibilities.

4.13.3 The Contractor shall implement the arrangements, and shall add to and otherwise change them, as desirable for its efficient performance.

4.13.4 The arrangements shall include systems, methods, planning and other preparations for providing personnel and resources, programming, recording, consultation, co-ordination, and co-operation, and for flexibility, as referred to in the Contract.

4.13.5 The Contractor shall keep the Employer's Representative fully informed about its current arrangements, in advance, and about their implementation.

4.13.6 The Contractor shall give the Employer's Representative all information, documents and records in the possession of, or available to, the Contractor or the Contractor's Personnel that the Employer's Representative requires to perform its functions and powers under the Contract.

Note
The Contractor must keep the Employer's Representative fully informed about all arrangements for the Works and provide the Employer's Representative with all the documents that he may need to carry out his function under the Contract.

4.14 Communications

4.14.1 The Parties intend all communications between them to be interpreted purposefully, having regard to the Contract's purposes.

4.14.2 Whenever any communication [including a notice, decision, objection, approval, certificate, determination, instruction or request] is to be given under the Contract it shall, unless the Contract provides otherwise, be in English, in writing and delivered as follows:

(1) for notices under clause 12 or clause 13, delivered by hand or sent by pre-paid registered post to the address for those notices in the Schedule, part 1A, as updated by the relevant Party

(2) for other communications, delivered by hand or sent by pre-paid post, fax or email according to the particulars for other communications in the Schedule, part 1A, as updated by the relevant Party.

4.14.3 Communications by pre-paid registered post are presumed to have been received at 10:00 a.m. two working days after posting. Fax and email communications are presumed to have been received when receipt is electronically recorded.

Note
All communications under the Contract must be in writing and delivered as follows:

(i) Clause 12 (Termination) and 13 (Disputes) must be delivered/sent by registered post to the address given in Part 1A of the Schedule;

(ii) Other communications must be delivered, posted, faxed or e-mailed to the relevant party according to the details in Part 1A of the Schedule.

Postal communications are presumed delivered at 10.00 hours, two working days after posting. This is important for ensuring compliance with the strict timetables set down in clauses 9 (Time and Completion) and 10 (Claims and Adjustments). Faxes or e-mails are presumed received when receipt is electronically recorded.

4.15 Meetings

4.15.1 The Contractor's representative and the Employer's Representative shall attend regular meetings scheduled by the Employer's Representative and any special meeting called by either of them to discuss a particular issue identified when calling the meeting. The Employer's Representative may invite other Employer's Personnel and the Contractor may invite Contractor's Personnel to attend meetings. The Contractor shall arrange for the attendance at a meeting of any Contractor's Personnel requested by the Employer's Representative. The time and place of meetings shall be set by the Employer's Representative, after consulting the Contractor, acting reasonably.

4.15.2 Within 5 working days after each meeting the Employer's Representative shall issue minutes of the meeting to the Employer and the Contractor. The Contractor shall notify the Employer's Representative of any objection to the minutes within 5 working days of receiving them, otherwise, unless clearly wrong, they shall be considered correct. Thereafter within 5 working days the Employer's Representative shall issue copies of the minutes and objections thereto to the Project Board Members, [and to the Standing Conciliator where appointed].

4.15.3 The dispute management procedure, under Clause 13 of the Contract, includes meetings of the Project Board. The Project Board shall only review disputes, formally referred to the Project Board, arising from sub-clauses 10.5.4 and 10.5.5 of the Contract

4.15.4 The Project Board is comprised of the individuals so identified to be members in the Schedule Part 3A of the Contract. Proposed changes to any of the individuals shall be communicated to all members of the Project Board in advance of any replacement being made. Replacement individuals to the Project Board shall have equivalent authority to reach agreement as their predecessor.

Note
Regular meetings shall take place between the Contractor and the Employer's Representative. Special meetings may be called and Employer's Personnel may be requested to attend. The Employer's Representative will issue the minutes within five working days of the meeting. The Contractor then has five working days to object to any minute and unless clearly wrong, the minutes are considered correct.

In the case of disputes, the procedures in relation to Project Board meetings are dealt with under Clause 13.

4.16 Confidentiality and Secrecy

4.16.1 The Contractor shall [and shall ensure that the Contractor's Personnel shall] keep confidential
(1) official information as defined in the Official Secrets Act 1963 and
(2) other information stated in the Works Requirements to be confidential or secret, or that the Employer or the Employer's Representative notifies the Contractor is confidential or secret.

4.16.2 The Employer shall keep confidential the Contractor's rates and prices in the Pricing Document or provided in accordance with the Contract, and any records given by the Contractor under the Contract that the Contractor notifies the Employer's Representative are confidential.

4.16.3 This sub-clause 4.16 shall not prevent disclosure of information, to the extent permitted by Law
(1) to the Contractor's Personnel, the Employer's Personnel or other professional advisors to the Contractor or Employer, who have first entered an undertaking in the terms of this sub-clause 4.16, to the extent necessary for the execution of the Works or to enforce the Contract or
(2) when required by Law or order of a court or, in the case of disclosure by the Employer, for governmental, parliamentary, statutory, administrative, fiscal or judicial purposes, or the publication of an award notice or
(3) that has, except as a result of breach of confidentiality, become available or generally known to the public at the time of the disclosure.

4.16.4 The Contractor's obligations under this sub-clause 4.16 shall be perpetual. The Employer's obligations under this sub-clause shall expire when the commercial sensitivity of the relevant information has ceased, in any event 5 years after the information was given.

Note
This is the confidentiality clause. Details of the Contractor's rates and Work Proposals are to be kept confidential by the Employer and the Employer's Representative. This sub-clause shall not prevent disclosure permitted by law, to enable Contractor to complete the Contract. The Contractor's obligation is perpetual. The Employer's obligation is limited to five years.

4.17 Contractor's Things Not to Be Removed

The Contractor shall submit details to the Employer's Representative before removing any Contractor's Things from the Site before the Employer's Representative issues a certificate of Substantial Completion of the Works or relevant Section.

Note
The Contractor must inform the Employer's Representative before he removes any of the Contractor's things from site before the Employer's Representative issues a Certificate of Substantial Completion. Contractor's things include equipment, facilities and other things the Contractor uses to execute the Works, except Works Items. Works Items means a part of the Works or anything the Contractor intends will become part of the Works and temporary works for the Works.

4.18 Contractor's Documents

All Contractor's Documents shall be in English, except when the Works Requirements or the Law specify another language

Note
Clause 4 sets out the manner in which this Contract will be managed and administered. The Contractor must appreciate the substantial management burden imposed on him by this Contract. Effective management and administration is essential and must be compliant with the requirements expressed under clause 4.

5 CONTRACTOR'S PERSONNEL

5.1 Contractor's Personnel to Carry Out Contractor's Obligations

The Contractor is liable for the acts and omissions of Contractor's Personnel [including Specialists and any design they do] as if they were the Contractor's acts and omissions.

5.2 Qualifications and Competence

The Contractor shall ensure that the Contractor's Personnel are suitably qualified and experienced and are competent to carry out their respective tasks.

5.3 Pay and Conditions of Employment

5.3.1 The Contractor shall prominently exhibit copies of this sub-clause 5.3 for the information of persons at the Site. In this clause 5 worker means an individual employed by, or otherwise working for, the Contractor or the Contractor's Personnel on or adjacent to the Site.

5.3.2 The Contractor shall ensure that the rates of pay and the conditions of employment, including pension contributions, comply with all applicable law and that those rates and conditions are at least as favourable as those for the relevant category of worker in any employment agreements registered under the Industrial Relations Acts 1946 to 2015. This applies to workers who are posted workers (within the meaning of Directive 96/71/EC of the European Parliament and the Council of the 16 December 1996 concerning the posting of workers in the framework provision of services), except that the Contractor's obligation to make pension contributions under registered employment agreements does not apply to posted workers who already contribute, or whose contributions are paid, to a supplementary pension scheme established in another member state of the European Union. The obligations in this sub- clause 5.3 apply regardless of what rates the Contractor has tendered for adjustments to the Contract Sum.

5.3.3 The Contractor shall in respect of

(i) workers employed by, or otherwise working for, the Contractor and

(ii) all other workers, ensure that their employers, or the persons for whom they are working,

do all of the following:

(1) pay all wages and other money due to each worker

(2) ensure that workers' wages are paid in accordance with the Payment of Wages Act 1991 and are never more than 1 month in arrears or unpaid

(3) pay all pension contributions and other amounts due to be paid on behalf of each worker

(4) make all deductions from payments to workers required by Law, and pay them on as required by Law

(5) keep proper records [including time sheets, wage books and copies of pay slips] showing the wages and other sums paid to and the time worked by each worker, deductions from each worker's pay and their disposition, and pension and other contributions made in respect of each worker, and produce these records for inspection and copying by any persons authorised by the Employer, whenever required by the Employer

(6) produce any other records relating to the rates of pay, pension and other contributions, deductions from pay and their disposition, conditions of employment of, rest periods, and annual leave for inspection and copying by any persons authorised by the Employer, whenever required by the Employer

(7) respect the right under law of workers to be members of trade unions

(8) observe, in relation to the employment of workers on the Site, the Safety, Health and Welfare at Work Act, 2005 and all employment law including the Employment

Equality Act 1998, the Industrial Relations Acts 1946 to 2004, the National Minimum Wage Act 2000, and regulations, codes of practice, legally binding determinations of the Labour Court and registered employment agreements under those Laws.

5.3.3A (1) Sub-clause 5.3.3A(2) shall only be included in the Contract if the Schedule, part 1J says so, and if not, neither sub-clause 5.3.3A(2) nor its omission shall be taken into account.

(2) The Employer shall be entitled to make random checks requiring production of records under sub-clauses 5.3.3(5) and (6).

5.3.4 If the Employer so requests, the Contractor shall, within 5 working days after the receipt of the request, give to the Employer a statement showing the amount of wages and other payments due at the date of the request to and in respect of each worker, or, in respect of workers not employed by or otherwise working for the Contractor, ensure that their employer or the person for whom they are working does the same.

5.3.5 The Employer may seek information under sub-clause 5.3.3 only for the purpose of ensuring the obligations referred to in this sub-clause 5.3 to workers have been properly discharged. All documents and records received under sub-clause 5.3.3 shall be returned to the person providing them or destroyed if the Employer is satisfied that the relevant employer has complied with legal obligations to workers.

5.3.6 If the Contractor has not complied with this sub-clause 5.3, the Employer shall [without limiting its other rights or remedies] be entitled to estimate the amount that should have been paid to workers and contributions that should have been made on their behalf, and the Employer may deduct the estimated amount from any payment due to the Contractor, until the Employer is satisfied that all proper amounts have been paid.

5.3.7 The Contractor shall give the Employer's Representative with each interim statement under sub-clause 11.1 a certificate in the form in the Works Requirements, that, in respect of the work to which the interim certificate relates, the Contractor has complied in full with this sub- clause 5.3.

5.3.8 If the Contractor does not comply with this sub-clause 5.3, it shall pay to the Employer any costs the Employer incurs in investigating and dealing with the non-compliance.

5.3.9 The Contractor shall ensure that in the event of an official of a trade union which is Party to a registered employment agreement affecting workers having concerns in relation to the Contractors or Contractor's Personnel's compliance with the agreement, that official will have access to a designated member of the Contractor's management who shall engage constructively to resolve all matters at this point.

Note

The Contractor shall ensure that the rates of pay and conditions of employment of each work person comply with applicable law and are no less favourable than those for the relevant category of work person in any employment agreement registered under the Industrial Relations Acts 1946–2004. The Contractor is also responsible for the compliance of subcontractors, including labour hire, with this condition. The Contractor is responsible for the enforcement of these requirements and any breach can be grounds for termination.

To confirm the Contractor's compliance with Condition 5.3, Condition 5.3.7 requires the Contractor to provide the Employer's Representative with a certificate (in the form in the Works Requirements) that the Contractor has complied in full with sub-clause 5.3. This certificate has to be submitted with each interim statement submitted by the Contractor under sub-clause 11.1 (Interim Payment); otherwise there will be no payment for the relevant Work Item until the certificate is given.

5.4 Subcontractors and Specialists

5.4.1 The Contractor shall not subcontract all of the Works to one or more Subcontractors. The Contractor shall submit details to the Employer's Representative of any proposed Specialist, other than one named in the Contract or when the Contract provides other procedures.

Note
The Contract allows for Named Subcontractors (Specialists). All Subcontractors will be engaged on a domestic basis. The Contractor has to obtain the acceptance of the Employer's Representative to any proposed Specialist. Clause 4.10 (Progress Reports).2 (2) also requires all Specialists and all off-site suppliers of the main Works item to be listed in the Progress Reports.

5.4.2 If Specialists or other Contractor's Personnel are named in the Contract, the Contractor shall ensure that they are engaged for and perform the work for which they are named.

Note
If the Specialist or other Contractor's personnel are named in the Employer's Work Requirements the Contractor shall ensure that they are engaged for the Works set out and named in the Contract.

The following pretender procedures will apply:

- The tender for the specialist work will be completed before the competition for the main Contract;
- The name of the Specialist, the subcontract price and the subcontract agreement will be included in the Works Requirements issued to tender.

The Employer should obtain an undertaking from the Specialist that he will enter into a subcontract with the Contractor on terms and obligations that apply under the main Contract. There is no right of objection from the Contractor as the Specialist is named in the tender document which he cannot alter and is therefore part of his bid.

5.4.3 If the Schedule, Part 3B names a Specialist, the following apply;

(i) where the Specialist's contract with the Employer is to be novated to the Contractor, (novated Specialist), and the Works Requirements includes a copy of that contract, the Contractor shall accept the novation, and the Parties shall, at the same time as entering the Agreement, enter the novation agreement. In the case of novated Specialists who were required to obtain a performance bond by the Employer, once the novation agreement is executed by the parties, the Employer shall write to the surety who has provided the performance bond to the novated Specialist informing them that they are assigning the benefit of that bond to the Contractor.

Note
Under Schedule Part 3B, the Employer has two options to appoint Specialists:

Option 1 is where the Employer may select a Specialist to be novated to the Contractor;

Option 2 is where the Employer has named a Reserve Specialist.

(ii) where the Contractor is to enter a sub-contract with a named Specialist, (Reserved Specialist), the Reserved Specialist sub-contract shall be an unamended form of sub- contract as identified in Schedule Part 1F(iii) and the Contractor shall enter into the sub-contract with the Reserved Specialist before the Starting Date.

Note
If the Work Requirements name a Specialist whose Contract is to be novated to the Contractor and includes a copy of the Contract, the Contractor shall accept the novation and execute the

novation agreement at the same time as the main Contract is executed. The process at tender stage is similar to 5.4.2 above. The Employer's Representative may not instruct the Contractor to enter into a subcontract with the Specialist selected by the Employer's Representative unless that Specialist was named in the Contract.

5.4.4 The Employer's Representative may not instruct the Contractor to enter a contract with a particular Specialist selected by the Employer's Representative unless the Specialist is named in the Contract (named Specialist).

5.4.5 The Contractor shall fully comply with its obligations under any contract with a Specialist and shall not terminate, allow to be terminated or accept a repudiation of such a contract without first submitting details to the Employer's Representative, except when an insolvency event, as set out in sub-clause 12.1, occurs in respect of the Specialist, or the Specialist has committed a serious breach of Law concerning safety, or the Specialist has failed to put or keep in effect insurance as required by the Specialist's contract. On any termination, the Contractor shall replace the Specialist, having submitted details of the replacement to the Employer's Representative. In the case of a named Specialist, referred to in sub-clause 5.4.3, the replacement Specialist proposed by the Contractor must meet minimum standards set out in the Works Requirements.

Note
The Contractor shall comply fully with the subcontract with the Specialist and cannot terminate without notifying the Employer's Representative except for insolvency or a serious breach of the law in relation to safety or a failure to comply with insurance requirements. On any termination the Contractor shall organise a replacement with a specialist approved by the Employer's Representative.

5.4.6 In addition to the reasons in sub-clause 4.7, the Employer's Representative may object to the proposed replacement of Contractor's Personnel because the proposed replacement does not have at least the level of experience, qualifications, competence, technical capacity, and financial standing of the person being replaced.

5.5 Collateral Warranties

If the Schedule, part 1F(i), states that a collateral warranty is required from any Specialist, before the date stated in the Schedule, the Contractor shall give the Employer a collateral warranty in the form included in the Works Requirements, or if there is none, a form approved by the Employer, executed by the Specialist and the Contractor. The minimum indemnity limit and maximum excess of professional indemnity insurance required of the Specialist shall be as stated in the Schedule, part 1F(i).

Note
This clause deals with collateral warranties. Note should be taken of the critical dates and the amounts that may be withheld from payments due to the Contractor for failure to meet those dates.

5.6 Removal of Workers

The Contractor shall remove from the Site any Contractor's Personnel that the Employer's Representative directs, because of the Contractor's Personnel's negligence or incompetence, or on the basis that the Contractor's Personnel's presence on the Site is not conducive to safety, health or good order.

5.7 Weekly Labour Records

Each Monday (or the next working day if Monday is not a working day) the Contractor shall give the Employer's Representative a list of the name of each worker who worked the week ending the previous Sunday and details of the category of and hours worked by each worker on the list.

5.8 Ancillary Certificates

If the Schedule, part 1F(ii) states that an Ancillary Certificate is required from the Contractor or the Contractor's Personnel, the Contractor shall obtain and provide to the Employer's Representative those Ancillary Certificates. [This does not limit the Contractor's obligation to provide all necessary Consents in accordance with sub-clause 2.3.1.]

Note

Sub-Clause 5.8 obliges the Contractor to provide the Ancillary Certificates for elements set out in the Schedule 1F. Contractors should ensure that those responsible for supply, design and or installation of those elements are made aware that Ancillary certificates will be required and failure to produce such Ancillary Certificates will result in delays to Substantial Completion of the Works.

General Notes on Clause 5

This clause sets out that the Contractor is liable for the acts and omissions of Contractor's Personnel (including Specialists and any design they do) as if they were the Contractor's acts and omissions.

This clause deals with the warranty with regard to experience and competence. It also introduces the strict requirements of Pay and Conditions of Employment. The Contractor's obligation to ensure compliance with the provisions extends to every work person engaged on or adjacent to the Site for the Contractor or his subcontractors and other persons assisting the Contractor to perform the Contract.

The Contract allows for the novation of contracts between the Employer and a Specialist to the Contractor. In this event the Contractor assumes the role and responsibilities of the Employer. Should a specialist be novated to the Contractor in this manner, the Contractor shall have no right to object to the appointment of the specialist.

6 PROPERTY

6.1 Ownership of Works Items

It is agreed, and the Contractor shall ensure, that each Works Item shall become the property of the Employer on the earliest of the following:

(1) when it is delivered to the Site, if owned by the Contractor
(2) when it is incorporated in the Works
(3) when any payment for the Works Item is made by the Employer to the Contractor.

Note
This sub-clause deals with ownership of Work Items and is particularly relevant to situations of insolvency. The Contractor is to ensure property passes to Employer when it is delivered to the site if owned by the Contractor. Work Items means a part of the Works, or anything that the Contractor intends will become part of the Works and temporary works for the Works.

6.2 Infringement of Property Rights

6.2.1 The Contractor shall indemnify the Employer against any liability resulting from any of the following infringing the property [including intellectual property] rights of any person:

(1) the Contractor's performance or non-performance of this Contract, unless the liability is covered by the Employer's indemnity in this sub-clause
(2) use of Works Items, Contractor's Things, or Contractor's Documents by
 (a) the Contractor or Contractor's Personnel or
 (b) the Employer or any other person to complete the Works following termination of the Contractor's obligation to complete the Works
(3) use by the Employer of the Works, Works Items, or the Contractor's Documents for the purpose for which they were given.

6.2.2 The Employer shall indemnify the Contractor against any liability resulting from any of the following infringing the property [including intellectual property] rights of any person:

(1) the unavoidable use by the Contractor, in accordance with the Contract, of the Works Requirements or Works Items or other things provided by the Employer
(2) the use or occupation by the Works of the Area Provided by the Employer (defined in sub-clause 7.1.1), when that is the unavoidable result of performing the Contract.

Note
Sub-clause 6.2 deals with indemnifying the Employer from infringement of property rights, including intellectual property rights.

6.3 Works Requirements

The Works Requirements shall remain the property of the Employer and the Contractor shall not use them [and shall ensure that the Contractor's Personnel do not use them] for any purpose other than to perform the Contract or to prosecute or defend a dispute under the Contract.

6.4 Rights in Contractor's Documents

6.4.1 The Employer may use, copy, modify, adapt and translate for any purpose in connection with the Works [including to construct, maintain, extend, use, operate, let, sell, promote, advertise, reinstate and repair the Works] the Contractor's Documents that are given, or, according to the Contract, must be given, to the Employer and the Works Proposals.

6.4.2 Where the Schedule, part 10, so states, all copyright and other rights in the Contractor's Documents that are prepared for the Works and are given, or according to the Contract, must be given, to the Employer and the Works Proposals transfers to the Employer when the Employer receives them.

6.4.3 The Contractor shall ensure that the Employer obtains the rights and interests described in this sub-clause 6.4.

6.4.4 The Contractor has no liability for the use of the Contractor's Documents for any purpose other than that for which they were given to the Employer.

Note
Sub-clause 6.4 deals with the property and rights in the Contractor's Documents, which the Employer has the right to use, copy, modify, adopt or translate for any purpose in connection with the Works. Part 1C of the Schedule may state that handover of copyright to the Employer and the Contractor shall ensure that all those rights can be transferred, including copyright to documents provided by Contractor's Personnel. The Contractor is not liable for the use of the Contractor's Documents for any purpose other than that for which they were provided to the Employer.

General Notes on Clause 6
This clause deals with Property Rights associated with the Works. The Employer wants to ensure that he will receive clear title to anything which will be incorporated into his building, and in this regard the Contractor is required to obtain clear title to items to be incorporated into the Works.

This clause provides that the Employer retains ownership of the Works Requirements, whilst he must obtain ownership of the Contractor's Documents should the Employer wish to exercise this option.

7 THE SITE

7.1 Lands Made Available for the Works

7.1.1 The Employer shall allow the Contractor to occupy and use each part of the area identified in the Works Requirements to be provided by the Employer (the **Area Provided by the Employer**) from a date on or before the latest of the following:

(1) the Starting Date

(2) the day after the Contractor has done what sub-clause 9.1 requires the Contractor to do before the Starting Date

(3) the date stated in the Works Requirements, if any

(4) the day after the Contractor has submitted its programme according to sub-clause 4.9

(5) the date stated for work to start on that part in the Contractor's current programme

(6) the date the Contractor actually requires the part in accordance with its actual progress.

7.1.2 The Contractor's right to occupy and use the Area Provided by the Employer or any part of it shall be subject to any limitations in the Works Requirements.

Note

Possession and access to the site will be subject to limitations as expressed in the Work Requirements.

7.1.3 The Contractor shall not be entitled to exclusive possession of the Area Provided by the Employer or any part of it and shall facilitate any occupation and use of it by the Employer and others stated in the Works Requirements. The Contractor's occupation and use of the Area Provided by the Employer shall be solely for the purpose of performing the Contract.

7.1.4 The Contractor's right to occupy and use a part of the Area Provided by the Employer shall end when the Employer's Representative certifies the Works or the relevant Section as Substantially Complete. After then the Employer shall allow the Contractor access to comply with sub-clause 8.6.1.

7.1.5 The Contractor's right to occupy and use a part of the Area Provided by the Employer shall end if the Employer takes over the relevant part of the Works under sub-clause 9.7.

7.1.6 The Contractor's right to occupy and use the Area Provided by the Employer shall end if the Contractor's obligation to complete the Works is terminated.

Note

The Employer shall allow access to the site on or before the latest of the following dates:

(i) The Starting Date—which is the date the Contractor proposes to start executing the Works on site, as notified by the Contractor to the Employer's Representative.

(ii) The day after the Contractor has done what sub-clause 9.1 (Starting Date) requires the Contractor to do before the Starting Date. This includes to:

- a Execute the Agreement;
- b Provide the performance bond;
- c Provide the parent company guarantee;
- d If it is required by the Contract execute the appointment of the Contractor as Project Supervisor;
- e Provide evidence that all insurances are in place;
- f Provide any Collateral Warranties (these may be supplied later with the agreement of the Employer's Representative).

(iii) The date stated in the Works Requirement.

(iv) The day after the Contractor has submitted its programme in accordance with sub-clause 4.9.
(v) The day stated for work to start on part of the site in the Contractor's current programme.
(vi) The date the Contractor actually requires the part in accordance with its actual programme.

The Contractor must insure all the Contract requirements are in place in advance of the Starting Date, otherwise the Employer does not have to give access to the site.

By sub-clause 7.1.3 the Contractor is not entitled to exclusive possession of the site.

7.2 Trespassers

After the Employer has allowed the Contractor to occupy and use any part of the Area Provided by the Employer, the Contractor shall be responsible for activities of trespassers, protesters and others, that are not Employer's Personnel on the Site, and the Employer shall have no responsibility to the Contractor for their activities or presence.

Note
The Contractor is responsible for trespassers and the Employer shall have no responsibility to the Contractor for their activities or presence. The Contractor will have to study the Work Requirements to establish if any parts of the site or facilities have to be operated and maintained during the course of the Works. Any costs involved will have to be built into the tender. In the event that facilities have to be operated the full extent of such should be determined as it could have serious implications on cost and resources.

7.3 Contractor Responsible for All Site Operations

The Contractor shall be responsible for all operations on the Site connected with the execution of the Works.

7.4 Services for Employer's Facilities

The Contractor shall operate and maintain parts of the Site and facilities of the Employer if the Works Requirements so require.

Note
The extent of what is meant by 'operate and' is new and would need to be carefully checked from the Work Requirements. Operate is not usually a 'Contractor' function so this could be a serious resource and cost issue.

7.5 Security and Safety of the Site and Nuisance

7.5.1 From and including the Starting Date until the Employer's Representative certifies the Works or the relevant Section as Substantially Complete, or the Employer takes over the relevant part of the Works under sub-clause 9.7, the Contractor shall do all of the following [without limiting other obligations]:

(1) be responsible for securing the Site and for keeping off the Site persons other than any of the following:
  (i) the Contractor's Personnel and the Employer's Personnel
  (ii) any other person notified to the Contractor by the Employer or the Employer's Representative as authorised to enter the Site

(iii) persons exercising public access to any roads, footpaths and areas on the Site

(iv) persons having a right to enter the Site under Legal Requirements

(2) keep the Site in good order and free from unnecessary obstructions

(3) take all necessary steps to secure the safety of all persons entitled to be on the Site and to protect users, owners and occupiers of land adjacent to the Site from hazards and interference arising from the Works [including providing any required fences, lighting, guarding, watching, roads and footpaths]

(4) take all necessary steps to ensure that the Contractor, the Contractor's Personnel and the execution of the Works do not do any of the following:

(i) unnecessarily cause a nuisance or inconvenience to the public or any user, owner or occupier of any land, road or footpath on or adjacent to the Site

(ii) unnecessarily interfere with the use of any such land, road or footpath.

7.5.2 The Employer shall ensure that Employer's Personnel on the Site comply with the Contractor's reasonable safety rules that have been notified to them by the Contractor.

7.5.3 This sub-clause 7.5 is subject to any exceptions in the Works Requirements

Note
This sub-clause deals with security and safety of site and nuisance, which are normal Contractor responsibilities. The Contractor has to permit the public to continue to exercise their right of public access to roads, footpaths and areas on the site.

7.6 Other Contractors

Where so stated in the Works Requirements, the Employer may arrange for work to be executed on the Site by Employer's Personnel. The Contractor shall co-operate with such Employer's Personnel and shall as far as practicable co-ordinate their activities with the execution of the Works.

Note
The Contractor has to allow access to the Employer's Personnel which are the Employer's Representative, the Employer's Employees, agents and consultants, other contractors of the Employer working on the site when acting within the scope of their contracts with the Employer, and, finally, anyone else the Employer's Representative advises the Contractor is an Employer's Personnel.

7.7 Setting Out the Works

The Contractor shall set out the Works by reference to the points, lines and levels of reference in the Works Requirements. The Contractor shall be responsible for the correct positioning of all parts of the Works and shall rectify any errors in the positions, levels, dimensions or alignment of the Works. Before setting out the Works the Contractor shall make all reasonable efforts to verify the accuracy of the setting out information in the Works Requirements.

Note
The Contractor is responsible for setting out the Works correctly by reference to the information provided in the Works Requirements. In the event that any changes to the information provided causes a change to the Work Requirements then it should be recorded by the Contractor, notified to the Employer's Representative and a Change Order be should be requested.

7.8 Archaeological Objects and Human Remains

If any fossils, coins, antiquities, monuments or other items of value or of archaeological or geological interest or human remains are discovered on or adjacent to the Site unless the Works Requirements say otherwise, the Contractor shall not disturb them, but shall take all necessary steps to preserve them, and shall promptly notify the Employer's Representative [and comply with any instructions]. As between the Parties, these items shall be the Employer's property.

Note
This clause sets out the steps the Contractor has to take in the event of archaeological objects or human remains been encountered on site. Item 18 of Section K of the Schedule, Part 1, provides for a Delay and Compensation Event in these circumstances, if elected by the Employer.

7.9 Access and Facilities

7.9.1 The Contractor [and not the Employer] shall be responsible for securing access to and through the Site and possession and use of any parts of the Site that are not the Area Provided by the Employer.

7.9.2 The Contractor [and not the Employer] shall be responsible for the suitability and availability of access routes to and within the Site, and any required maintenance or upgrading of them, and any charges for use of them.

7.9.3 The Contractor shall take all reasonable steps to ensure that its traffic [including Contractor's Personnel's traffic]

(1) complies with the restrictions concerning laden weight and dimensions in the Law and

(2) does not damage roads [except for ordinary wear], bridges or other property.

7.9.4 The Contractor shall also be responsible for obtaining any additional facilities, and for providing all power, water and other services it requires to perform the Contract.

Note
The Contractor is responsible for securing access to and through the Site and the suitability and availability of access routes to the Site, within the site, including upgrading, maintenance and paying any charges arising. He is to take all reasonable steps to ensure traffic safety, complying with the current 'Road Traffic (Construction Equipment Use of Vehicles) Regulations' and not to damage roads, bridges or other property.

7.10 Condition of Site on Completion

As soon as practicable after the Works or any Section reaches Substantial Completion, the Contractor shall remove from the Site Contractor's Things not required to perform the Contractor's remaining obligations, and leave the Works or Section in an orderly manner. At the end of the Defects Period, the Contractor shall remove from the Site any remaining Contractor's Things. In this sub-clause 7.10, Contractor's Things includes temporary works that have not become part of the Works.

Note
This sub-clause requires the Contractor, on leaving the site on completion, to remove the Contractor's Things which are not required to complete obligations, and to leave in an orderly manner, and at the end of the Defects Period to remove any remaining Contractor's Things.

7.11 Working Times

The Contractor shall ensure that the Contractor's Personnel work on the Site only during the working times set out in the Works Requirements, if any, unless

(1) there is imminent danger to safety or health or of damage to the Works or other property or

(2) otherwise agreed with the Employer's Representative.

Note

This sub-clause makes it a condition to keep within legal working hours as set down in planning consents or other documents where they are set out in Work Requirements, unless there is imminent danger to health and safety or damage to Works or to property or it is otherwise agreed with the Employer's Representative.

General Notes on Clause 7

This clause sets out the obligations of the Parties in relation to delivery and occupation of the Site. The Employer is required to deliver the Site, or any part of it, to the Contractor by, at the latest, the date upon which the Contractor actually requires the part of the site in accordance with actual progress. The Contractor will not obtain exclusive possession of the Site or any part of it. This clause places the responsibility for trespassers with the Contractor. The only people who will be contractually compelled to abide by the Contractor's safety rules will be the Employer's and Contractor's Personnel.

The Contractor, from the Starting Date, becomes entirely responsible for all operations on the Site (Clause 7.5.1) and for safety and security.

The Contractor is responsible for setting out in accordance with the Works Requirements. The Contractor will also be required to take care of archaeological finds, should the Employer so elect under Item 18 of the Schedule, Part 1K.

The Contractor is responsible for access routes, traffic and utilities required for the execution of the Works. On completion of the Works, the Contractor shall remove Contractor's Things from the Site (including Temporary Works). The clause also provides that the Works will only be undertaken during pre-specified Working Times.

8 QUALITY, TESTING AND DEFECTS

8.1 Standards of Workmanship and Works Items

The Contractor shall ensure all of the following:

(1) that the Works are executed and completed

  (i) in accordance with all the requirements in, and reasonably inferred from, the Contract [including, where so required by the Contract, in accordance with Contractor's Documents that have been submitted to the Employer's Representative] and

  (ii) in a proper and workmanlike manner and using good practice

(2) that all Works Items [whether or not the Contractor is required to select them]

  (i) comply with the Contract and the Legal Requirements and

  (ii) are of good quality and, unless the Contract provides otherwise, new.

(3) that all materials and goods that are Works Items [whether or not the Contractor is required to select them] are fit for the purpose for which they are normally used

(4) that all Works Items selected or designed by the Contractor [including by any Specialist] are fit for their intended purpose in the Works.

Note
All materials and goods are to be new and of good quality unless otherwise provided in the Work Requirements.

8.2 Quality Assurance

The Contractor shall establish and implement quality assurance procedures as required by the Works Requirements, including procedures for establishing quality assurance systems for itself and Subcontractors. The quality assurance procedures shall be reflected in appropriate quality plans submitted to the Employer's Representative. The Contractor shall give the Employer's Representative copies of all reports prepared in accordance with the Contractor's quality assurance procedures. The Employer's Representative may monitor, spot check and audit the Contractor's quality assurance procedures.

Note
Sub-clause 8.2 deals with the expected quality assurance procedures that the Contractor shall establish. The Employer's Representative is entitled to a copy of the Contractor's quality assurance plan and all reports prepared by the Contractor. The Employer's Representative is entitled to monitor, audit and spot check the Contractor's quality assurance procedure.

8.3 Inspection

8.3.1 The Contractor shall ensure that the Employer's Representative, Assigned Certifier, and anyone authorised by the Employer's Representative, is able at all reasonable times to have access to all places where the Works are being executed [whether or not at the Site] and any place where any Works Items are produced, stored, extracted or prepared, or any other obligation of the Contractor under the Contract is being performed, and are able there to inspect, test, observe and examine all such items and activities.

8.3.2 The Contractor shall promptly give the Employer's Representative and the Assigned Certifier all particulars the Employer's Representative and the Assigned Certifier requests about the mode, place and time of manufacture, the source of supply and the performance capabilities of Works Items and any related information, including any test certificates that the Contract provides for.

8.3.3 The Contractor shall notify the Employer's Representative and the Assigned Certifier before any Works Item is covered or any Works Item that is to be inspected is packed or made impossible or difficult to inspect, in either case giving the Employer's Representative, and any person authorised by the Employer's Representative, a reasonable opportunity to inspect the Works Item.

Note
The Contractor is to give the Employer's Representative notice of when Work Items that require inspection are being covered up or packaged or made impossible or difficult to inspect. The Contractor shall notify the Employer's Representative and provide a reasonable opportunity for the inspection to take place.

8.4 Tests

8.4.1 The Contractor shall supply all Contractor's Things, documents, information, suitably qualified and experienced personnel, power, consumables and instruments required to carry out tests that the Contract [including the Inspection Plan] requires the Contractor to do [both before and after Substantial Completion]. The Contractor shall agree with the Employer's Representative and the Assigned Certifier the time and place for these tests. The Employer's Representative, and others authorised by the Employer, may attend and observe the tests, and the Contractor shall facilitate their attendance and observation. Regardless of whether any Employer's Personnel attends, the Contractor shall promptly give the Employer's Representative a certified report of the result of every test.

8.4.2 If a test is failed, the Contractor may elect to repeat the test, or the Employer's Representative may require that the test be repeated. The Contractor shall, on request, pay the Employer any costs the Employer incurs as a result of any re-testing.

8.4.3 If the Contractor rectifies a Defect, it shall repeat any relevant test the Contract specifies for the relevant Works Item, if the Employer's Representative so directs.

Note
This sub-clause deals with the carrying out of all tests which the Contractor is required by the Contract to do, both before and after Substantial Completion. The Contractor is to facilitate the attendance of the Employer's Representative to observe the tests, and to provide certified reports of result of each test. If a test fails the Contractor may elect to retest or be instructed by the Employer's Representative. The Contractor is responsible for the Employer's costs arising from any retest. If the Contractor repairs a defect for which he is at fault he shall repeat any relevant test to that Work if so requested by the Employer's Representative at the Contractor's cost.

8.5 Defects

8.5.1 The Employer's Representative may direct the Contractor to search for a Defect or suspected Defect or its cause. This may include uncovering, dismantling, re-covering and re-erecting work, providing facilities for tests, testing and inspecting. If, through searching or otherwise, the Contractor discovers a Defect, the Contractor shall notify the Employer's Representative as soon as practicable.

8.5.2 If, through notification or otherwise, the Employer's Representative becomes aware of a Defect, the Employer's Representative may direct the Contractor to do any of the following [or any combination of them]:

(1) to remove the Works Item with the Defect from the Site
(2) to demolish the Works Item with the Defect, if incorporated in the Works
(3) to reconstruct, replace or correct the Works Item with the Defect
(4) not to deliver the Works Item with the Defect to the Site.

8.5.3 The Contractor shall comply with any direction under this sub-clause 8.5 within the reasonable times, if any, the Employer's Representative directs. If the Contractor fails to begin the work required to comply with the direction within the reasonable time directed, if any, or to complete it as soon as practicable, the Employer may have the work done by others and the Contractor shall, on request, pay the Employer its cost of doing so.

8.5.4 Alternatively, the Contractor and the Employer's Representative may, with the Employer's consent, agree that the Employer will accept the Defect, either in whole or subject to any change to the Works Requirements that the Employer's Representative directs. In this case, the Contract Sum shall be reduced by the amount that, in the opinion of the Employer's Representative, is the resulting decrease in the value of the Works to the Employer. If the Employer's Representative notifies the Contractor that the Employer will not accept a Defect, this shall be conclusive.

8.5.5 If a Defect deprives the Employer of substantially the whole benefit of the Works or any Section or other material part of the Works, the Employer's Representative may reject the Works or the relevant part of the Works (as the case may be) and [without limiting the Employer's other rights], the Contractor shall pay the Employer all sums the Employer has paid the Contractor for the Works or the relevant part, together with the Employer's financing costs and the cost of dismantling and removing the Works, clearing the Site and returning the Works Items to the Contractor.

8.5.6 The Employer's Representative may give a direction or rejection under this sub-clause 8.5 at any time before the Defects Certificate is issued. [The Contractor shall not be entitled to any adjustment to the Contract Sum or extension of time because of a direction given to deal with, or as a result of, a Defect or any other breach of the Contract by the Contractor.]

Note

This sub-clause deals with defects which now includes all workmanship and materials and Contractor's documentation which may not be in accordance with the Contract. In dealing with a defect there are five options open to the Employer's Representative:

(i) Remove the Work Item with defect from the site;
(ii) Demolish Work Item with defect if incorporated in Works;
(iii) Reconstruct, replace or correct the Works with the defect;
(iv) Not deliver the Work Items with the defect to the site;
(v) Alternatively, the Employer's Representative and the Contractor, with the Employer's agreement, may accept the defect either in whole or subject to any change in Work Requirements instructed by the Employer's Representative. Any resulting decrease in value of the Works shall be determined by the Employer's Representative and the amount shall be deducted from the Contract Sum. Such deduction may not relate solely to cost alone.

If the Employer's Representative will not accept a defect it shall be conclusive under this Contract.

The Employer's Representative may reject the Works or part of the Works if the defect denies the Employer of, substantially, the whole benefit of the Works or part thereof. The Contractor shall pay the Employer all sums paid to the Contractor by the Employer for those Works or the part of the Works rejected, together with the Employer's financing costs, the cost of dismantling the Works and removing from the site, and the costs of returning Work Items to the Contractor.

No adjustment to cost or time are allowed for a defect which is the fault of the Contractor.

8.6 Defects Period

8.6.1 As soon as practicable after Substantial Completion of the Works or any Section, the Contractor shall complete any outstanding work and rectify any Defects that the Employer's Representative directs before the end of the Defects Period. In doing so, and in doing any tests after Substantial Completion, the Contractor shall cause as little disruption as possible to occupants and users of the Works.

8.6.2 If work remains outstanding or Defects remain uncorrected at the end of the Defects Period, or if the Contractor has completed outstanding work or rectified Defects after Substantial Completion of the Works or relevant Section and before the end of the Defects Period, the Employer's Representative may [without limiting the Employer's other rights] make an appropriate extension to the Defects Period. With the Employer's agreement the Employer's Representative may, at the time that the Defects Period would have ended without this extension, issue an interim payment certificate conclusively making an appropriate reduction in retention, and the Contractor shall be entitled to invoice the Employer for that amount.

Note
Sub-clause 8.6 deals with the remedy of defects in the Defects Period. The Employer's Representative may, where serious defects have occurred during the Defects Period, seek to have the period extended to monitor the defects. The Contractor may agree and there will be an appropriate reduction to retention at the original defects completion date.

If no extension is agreed the Employer's Representative may, at the end of Defects Period, assess the risk that defects in the Work Item concerned may occur or be noticed in the period from the remedial work to the Works Item and equal in length to the Defects Period, and make an appropriate deduction to the Contract Sum to compensate the Employer for that risk.

Sub-clause 8.6.2 (Defects Period) entitles the Employer's Representative to reduce the Contract Sum to compensate the Employer against the risk of defects occurring in the future.

8.7 Defects Certificate

The Employer's Representative shall issue the Defects Certificate to the Contractor and the Employer within 20 working days after the end of the Defects Period. [Nothing in this clause 8, nor any exercise or non-exercise by the Employer or the Employer's Representative of their rights under this clause 8, nor the Defects Certificate, relieves the Contractor of any obligation, except to the extent that a Defect is accepted by agreement under sub-clause 8.5.4.]

Note
The Defects Certificate means a certificate of the Employer's Representative issued to certify that the Defects Period has ended. The Employer's Representative shall issue this certificate to the Contractor and the Employer within 20 working days after the end of the Defects Period.

General Note on Clause 8
The Works Requirements will contain quality assurance procedures. The Contractor should establish and implement these requirements. The quality assurance procedures shall be reflected in the appropriate documents that the Contractor submits to the Employer's Representative. The Employer's Representative may monitor, carry out spot checks and audit the Contractor's quality assurance procedures.

The Defects Period means the period starting on Substantial Completion of the Works and continuing for the period stated in the Schedule, Part 1, Section I (which, if none is stated, should taken to be one year) as may be extended under clause 8.6.2.

In the event that the Contractor does not agree with the amount of the reduction to the Contract Sum the Contractor can refer the issue to conciliation under sub-clause 13.1.

Where the Defects Period is extended there will also be issues with the release of the bond and maintaining insurances on the project. The Contractor will have to inform his bondsman and insurance agents.

9 TIME AND COMPLETION

9.1 Starting Date

9.1.1 The Contractor shall set the Starting Date, giving the Employer's Representative at least 15 working days notice, or any shorter period the Employer's Representative may agree, or any different period stated in the Works Requirements. The Starting Date shall, unless otherwise stated in the Works Requirements, be no more than 20 working days after the Contract Date.

9.1.2 Before the Starting Date [unless already given by the Contractor before the Contract Date, for example in response to a letter of intent] the Contractor shall give the Employer all of the following, all executed, as relevant, by the relevant persons:

(1) the Agreement
(2) a performance bond, if required by the Contract
(3) a parent company guarantee, if required by the Contract
(4) if the Works Requirements state that the Contractor or the Contractor's nominee is to be appointed as project supervisor for the construction stage, the required appointment, and the developed safety and health plan required by the Construction Regulations
(5) evidence that the insurances required by the Contract are in effect
(6) any collateral warranties required by the Contract
(7) copies of signed agreements and unamended form of sub-contract as identified in Schedule Part 1F(iii)

However, collateral warranties may be given on a later date that the Employer's Representative has agreed to.

9.1.3 On the Starting Date, the Contractor shall start to execute the Works on the Site. The Contractor shall, unless the Employer's Representative directs otherwise, proceed regularly and diligently in order to achieve Substantial Completion of the Works and each Section by its Date for Substantial Completion.

Note

Sub clause 9.1 deals with the Starting Date. Notice of at least 15 working day must be given to the Employer's Representative, or any shorter period agreed or as per the Work Requirements.

Unless it is otherwise stated in the Work Requirements, the Starting Date shall be no later than 20 working days after the Contract Date.

The Contractor must comply with the following obligations before the Starting Date:

(i) Executing the Agreement;
(ii) Providing the performance bond, if required;
(iii) Providing parent company guarantees, if required;
(iv) If required under the Work Requirements, confirming acceptance of the appointment as project supervisor for the construction stage, and providing a copy of the developed health and safety plan;
(v) Providing evidence that the insurances required by the Contract is in place;
(vi) Providing collateral warranties required, though they may be deferred to later date by the Employer's Representative, or as per the Schedule;
(vii) Provide copies of all relevant completed Sub-Contracts as set out in the Schedule Part 1 F (iii).

It is possible that Works could be delayed for want of sufficient time to serve a statutory notice. It may be necessary to work under a Letter of Intent as contained in the Model Forms. The Contractor should ensure that any Letter of Intent provides for the Contractor to be paid for all Works and documents produced in the event that the project is delayed or cancelled.

9.2 Suspension

9.2.1 The Employer's Representative may at any time direct the Contractor to suspend all or part of the work under the Contract. The Contractor shall comply with the direction and, during suspension, shall protect, store and secure the affected Works Items against deterioration, loss and damage and maintain the Insurances.

9.2.2 After a suspension under clause 9.2.1, the Contractor shall resume work when so directed by the Employer's Representative. When a direction to resume is given, the Contractor and the Employer's Representative shall jointly examine the Works and Works Items affected by the suspension. If the Contractor is entitled to an adjustment of the Contract Sum or an extension of time because of the suspension, the Contractor's cost of rectifying any deterioration in or loss of the Works or Work Items that the Contractor could not have avoided shall be included in the determination of the adjustment, and any resulting delay shall be taken into account in determining the extension.

9.2.3 If a suspension, that did not result from a breach of the Contractor's obligations, has continued for more than 3 months, the Contractor may request the Employer's Representative's permission to proceed. If the Employer's Representative does not give permission within 28 days after being requested to do so, the Contractor may, by giving notice to the Employer's Representative

(1) if the suspension affects part of the Works, treat the suspension as a Change Order to omit that part of the Works or

(2) if the suspension affects the whole of the Works, give notice to terminate the Contractor's obligation to complete the Works under the Contract.

Note

The Employer may suspend the Works. In the event of a suspension the Works have to be protected, stored and kept secure. The Works will be resumed on instruction from the Employer's Representative. The Contractor is entitled to the cost of any remedial works. The Contractor is entitled to an adjustment of the Contract Sum and an extension of time, both of which have to be assessed.

Suspension under 9.2 is a Delay and Compensation Event (Item 3 of the Schedule, Part 1, Section K). Costs are calculated at the daily delay rate quoted by the Contractor in the Schedule (Part 2, Section E). These costs may not cover the Contractor's full costs, e.g. costs from subcontractors and offsite storage, etc.

If the suspension lasts more than 3 months then the Contractor may treat the instruction to suspend as an instruction to omit that part of the Works or give notice to terminate the Contractor's obligations under the Contract.

9.3 Delay and Extension of Time

9.3.1 If the Contractor becomes aware that work under the Contract is being or is likely to be delayed for any reason, it shall as soon as practicable notify the Employer's Representative of the delay and its cause. As soon as practicable after that, and in any event within 40 working days after the Contractor became aware of the delay, the Contractor shall give the Employer's Representative full details of the delay and its effect on the progress of the Works. But if the Contractor has given notice and details of the delay under sub-clause 10.3.1 it does not have to give notice or details again under this sub-clause 9.3.1 for the same delay. In any event, the Contractor shall promptly give any further information about the delay the Employer's Representative directs.

Note
Sub-clause 9.3 is a critical clause. In order to retain any rights to receive extensions and costs to cover resulting delay, the Contractor's organisation needs to follow it to the letter.

Under sub-clause 9.3.1, where the Contractor is aware that the work is being or is likely to be delayed for any reason, he shall, as soon as is practicable, notify the Employer's Representative of the delay and cause.

At 40 working days, at the most, after the event he shall give to the Employer's Representative full details of delay and its effect on progress and promptly supply any further information on the delay requested by the Employer's Representative.

Note that this means any delay, not just those to which an entitlement to an extension of time is given.

9.3.2 If Substantial Completion of the Works or any Section has been, is being or will be delayed beyond the Date for Substantial Completion by a Delay Event and if all of the following apply:

(1) the Delay Event is not a result of the Contractor's or Contractor's Personnel's act or omission or the Contractor's breach of the Contract
(2) the Contractor makes all reasonable efforts to avoid and minimise the delay
(3) the Contract does not provide otherwise

then, subject to this sub-clause 9.3, sub-clause 9.4 and clause 10, there shall be an extension to the Date for Substantial Completion of the Works and any affected Section equal to the amount of the delay beyond the Date for Substantial Completion caused by the Delay Event taking into account only Site Working Days. The Contractor and the Employer's Representative shall follow the procedure in clause 10.

Note
Sub-clause 9.3.2.deals with delay to the Substantial Completion Date of whole or part of the Works which has been, is being or will be affected. The delays must not be the result of an act, omission or breach of Contract by the Contractor. The Delay Event must be one that could not be avoided. The Contractor has to make all reasonable efforts to mitigate the delay.

The clause states that subject to sub clause 9.3 and 9.4 there shall be an extension to the Substantial Completion Date of the whole or the section equal to the amount of delay taking into account site working days only.

The Employer's Representative may act on his own initiative in that he does not need to wait for notice if he considers an extension is due. This is, we presume, to protect the Employer's right to an extension of time.

All claims for extensions of time must be processed under clause 10.3. Failure to do so will defeat any entitlement.

9.3.3 The Employer's Representative may, at any time, revise a determination of an extension to the Date for Substantial Completion of the Works or any Section, but shall not bring those dates forward except by agreement with the Contractor under sub-clause 9.5 when work has been omitted.

Note
Under sub-clause 9.3.3 the Employer's Representative may review an assessment at any time but may not bring the Substantial Completion Date forward except with the Contractor's agreement under sub-clause 9.5 where works are omitted.

9.4 Programme Contingency

9.4.1 In sub-clause 9.4.3

- references to the **first threshold** or **T1** and to the **second threshold** or **T2** are to the first threshold and the second threshold in the Schedule, part 1K
- references to **delay** or **D** are to the total number of Site Working Days' delay to Substantial Completion of the Works caused by Compensation Events for which the Contractor would otherwise be entitled to an extension and Delay Cost, but for this sub- clause 9.4
- references to **extensions** or **E** are to the total of extensions to the initial Date for Substantial Completion of the Works for delay caused by Compensation Events for which the Contractor is entitled to Delay Cost.

9.4.2 The Contractor has included in the initial Contract Sum and shall include in its programme a contingency for delays to the Date for Substantial Completion of the Works caused by Compensation Events.

9.4.3 The programme contingency is applied to derive extensions as follows:

(1) Unless delay exceeds the first threshold, there are no extensions.

(2) If delay exceeds the first threshold but is less than or equals the sum of the first threshold and twice the second threshold, extensions equal half of the result obtained by subtracting the first threshold from delay.

(3) If delay is more than the sum of the first threshold and twice the second threshold, extensions equal delay minus the first threshold minus the second threshold.

[This can be expressed by the following rules:

Rule 1:	If $D \leq T1$	then	$E = 0$
Rule 2:	If $T1 < D$ but $\leq (T1+2T2)$	then	$E = \frac{(D - T1)}{2}$
Rule 3:	If $D > (T1+2T2)$	then	$E = D - T1 - T2$

For example, if the first threshold (T1) is 20 Site Working Days and the second threshold (T2) is 30 Site Working Days

— if delay (D) is 10 Site Working Days, the Contractor would be entitled to no extensions, applying rule 1

— if delay (D) is 28 Site Working Days, the Contractor would be entitled to 4 Site Working Days' extensions, applying rule 2

— if delay (D) is 38 Site Working Days, the Contractor would be entitled to 9 Site Working Days' extensions, applying rule 2

— if delay (D) is 90 Site Working Days, the Contractor would be entitled to 40 Site Working Days' extensions, applying rule 3.]

9.4.4 [This sub-clause 9.4 does not apply to extensions to the Date for Substantial Completion of a Section, nor to extensions of time resulting from Delay Events that are not Compensation Events.]

9.4.5 Use of the programme contingency provided for in this sub-clause shall be claimed and determined in accordance with this clause 9 and clause 10. Programme contingency may be drawn-down when Substantial Completion has been, is being, or will be delayed beyond the Date for Substantial Completion minus the unused part of the first and second thresholds. In making a determination under sub-clauses 9.3 and 10.5 in respect of a delay to Substantial Completion of the Works, the Employer's Representative shall notify the Contractor and the Employer of how much of the first threshold and the second threshold have been used-up by delays to Substantial Completion of the Works caused by Compensation Events.

Note
This condition provides the Employer the opportunity to 'buy out' a numbers of days' delay. This is referred to as the 'programme contingency'. The contingency for delays has to be built into the programme time and the associated costs have to be included in the tender sum. The amount of contingency days will be given to the Contractor in the Schedule, Part 1K, at tender stage. Before an extension of time is granted the days in the threshold contingency must be exceeded.

The delays must arise from Compensation Events only. The Compensation Events will be detailed by the Employer in the Schedule, Part 1, Section K.

The Contractor records and provides to the Employer's Representative details of the delays and their affect. The Employer's Representative makes the final assessment under clause 10.5.

The Employer's Representative shall notify the Contractor and the Employer of how much of the threshold is used up by the delays to the Date for Substantial Completion caused by Compensation Events.

Condition 9.4.3 refers to the first and second thresholds. This sub-clause sets out in detail the operation of the two thresholds and how they are to be dealt with.

9.5 Omissions and Reduction of Time

If a Change Order omits any of the Works, and the omission will result, or has resulted, in a reduction of the time required to complete the Works or any Section, the Date for Substantial Completion shall be reduced by any amount agreed between the Employer's Representative and the Contractor. [If there is no agreement, there shall be no reduction.]

Note
The Date for Substantial Completion can be brought forward as a result of a Change Order arising from an omission. The reduction in the Contract time to complete the Works has to be agreed with the Contractor; without agreement the Date for Substantial Completion cannot be brought forward.

9.6 Substantial Completion

9.6.1 The Contractor shall achieve Substantial Completion of the Works and each Section by its Date for Substantial Completion.

9.6.2 Within 20 working days after receiving the Contractor's request to certify Substantial Completion of the Works or a Section, the Employer's Representative shall give to the Contractor and the Employer

(1) a certificate stating the date that Substantial Completion occurred or

(2) the reasons for not issuing the certificate.

But if the Schedule, part 1H, so states, the Employer's Representative shall not be required to certify Substantial Completion of the Works or a Section before its Date for Substantial Completion. The certificate may include a list of Defects and any outstanding work [but nothing in the certificate, including the failure to list any Defect, relieves the Contractor of any obligations].

Note
The Contractor must request the Employer's Representative to issue a Certificate of Substantial Completion for the Works or a Section of the Works. The Employer's Representative has 20 working days after receiving the request to issue the certificate stating the date that Substantial Completion was achieved or to state the reasons for not issuing the certificate. Part 1H of the Schedule can state that the Employer's Representative does not have to issue the Certificate for a date earlier than the Substantial Completion Date stated in the Contract.

The certificate may include a list of defects or incomplete works that the Contractor has to make good or complete.

9.7 Taking Over Part of the Works

9.7.1 The Employer may take over a part of the Works before Substantial Completion of the Works or any Section including the part, provided that the Employer's Representative first issues a notice to the Contractor at least 5 working days before the Employer intends to take over the part, the notice stating all of the following:

(1) the part to be taken over by the Employer
(2) any work remaining to be completed in that part
(3) the value, when it gets to Substantial Completion, of the part to be taken over and the proportion of the Contract Sum that this value represents
(4) the date the part will be taken over.

9.7.2 The Contractor shall have no liability for delay in completing the part to be taken over occurring after the date stated in the notice. The rate of liquidated damages for delay in achieving Substantial Completion of the Works and any relevant Section shall reduce by a fraction equal to the fraction of the Contract Sum represented by the Contract value of the part of the Works taken over, as certified by the Employer's Representative. The retention amount to be withheld under sub-clause 11.3 from interim payments until Substantial Completion shall reduce by the same fraction.

9.8 Liquidated Damages

9.8.1 If the Works do not reach Substantial Completion by the Date for Substantial Completion of the Works, the Contractor shall pay the Employer [and the Employer may deduct from payments to the Contractor] liquidated damages calculated at the rate stated in the Schedule, part 1G, for the period from the Date for Substantial Completion of the Works to the date of substantial completion of the Works.

9.8.2 If a Section does not reach Substantial Completion by its Date for Substantial Completion, the Contractor shall pay to the Employer liquidated damages calculated at the rate stated in the Schedule for the period from the Date for Substantial Completion of the Section to the date of substantial completion of the Section (or, if earlier and if the Schedule states a rate of liquidated damages for the Works, to the Date for Substantial Completion of the Works).

9.8.3 In this sub-clause 9.8 **date of substantial completion** means the date certified by the Employer's Representative that the Works or Section reached Substantial Completion.

Note
If the Works do not reach Substantial Completion by the stated date the Contractor shall pay the Employer, or the Employer may deduct from payments due to the Contractor, liquidated damages calculated at the rate stated in Part 1G of the Schedule. Liquidated damages may also apply to a section or sections of the Works.

In the event that the Employer's Representative does not issue the certificate of Substantial Completion as a result of incomplete works as advised in accordance with clause 9.6.2(2) then the Contractor is exposed to liquidated damages from the Employer.

General Notes on Clause 9
Delay and Extension of Time: The Contractor shall, as soon as he becomes aware that the Works are being or are likely to be delayed, must notify the Employer's Representative of the delay and

the cause. Within 40 days after becoming aware of the delay the Contractor shall provide full details of the delay and the effect on progress of the Works to the Employer's Representative.

While Condition 9.3.1 requires the Contractor to give notice of delay to the Employer's Representative, the claim for the extension of time and/or costs must be given under Condition 10.3.1, and any notice under 10.3.1 must prominently state that it is being given under Condition 10.3.

The time restraints, i.e. 40 working days after the Contractor became aware of the delay (not the notice), must be strictly adhered to.

Conditions 9.3 (Delay Events), 4.8 (Programme), 4.9 (Progress Reports) and 10.3 are closely related.

The Employer's Representative extends the Date for Substantial Completion under sub-clause 9.3.2.

In the event that a Contractor has already provided a notice and details of a delay for an event under Condition 10.3.1 the Contractor does not have to give a notice under Condition 9.3.1 for the same delay.

10 CLAIMS AND ADJUSTMENTS

10.1 Compensation Event

10.1.1 Subject to and in accordance with this sub-clause 10.1, if a Compensation Event occurs the Contract Sum shall be adjusted [upward or downward] by the amount provided in sub-clause 10.6. However, if the adjustment is an increase it shall only take effect to the extent that all of the following apply to the Compensation Event:

(1) The Compensation Event is not a result of the Contractor's or Contractor's Personnel's act or omission or the Contractor's breach of the Contract

(2) The Contractor makes all reasonable efforts to avoid and minimise the adverse effects of the Compensation Event.

(3) The Contractor has complied with this clause 10 in full [including giving notices and details within the time required]

(4) The Contract does not provide otherwise.

10.1.2 The Contractor's sole remedies for a Compensation Event shall be those stated in the Contract.

10.2 Contractor to Pay Employer's Cost of Checking Quantities

The Contractor shall pay the Employer's cost of having a check done if the Contractor calls for an adjustment to the Contract Sum because of a difference between the Contract value of the Works according to the quantities and descriptions in a Bill of Quantities (if any) in the Pricing Document and the Contract value of the Works according to the Works Requirements (when this is a Compensation Event), and it is found that no increase is to be made to the Contract Sum.

10.3 Contractor Claims

10.3.1 If the Contractor considers that under the Contract there should be an extension of time or an adjustment to the Contract Sum, or that it has any other entitlement under or in connection with the Contract, the Contractor shall, as soon as practicable and in any event within 20 working days after it became aware, or should have become aware, of something that could result in such an entitlement, give notice of this to the Employer's Representative. The notice must be given according to sub-clause 4.14 and prominently state that it is being given under sub-clause 10.3 of the Contract. Within a further 20 working days after giving the notice, the Contractor shall give the Employer's Representative details of all of the following:

(1) all relevant facts about the claim

(2) a detailed calculation and, so far as practicable, a proposal, based on that calculation, of any adjustment to be made to the Contract Sum and of the amount of any other entitlement claimed by the Contractor

(3) if the Contractor considers that the programme contingency referred to in sub-clause 9.4 should be used or that there should be an extension of time, the information required under sub-clause 9.3, and, so far as practicable, a proposal, based on that information for any use of the programme contingency or any extension to the Date for Substantial Completion of the Works and any affected Section.

The Contractor shall give any further information about the event or circumstance requested by the Employer's Representative.

10.3.2 If the Contractor does not give notice and details in accordance with and within the time provided in this sub-clause 10.3, except where the Contractor has been required to and has given a proposal complying in full with sub-clause 10.4 [notwithstanding anything else in the Contract] the Contractor shall not be entitled to an increase to the Contract Sum or extension of time or use of the programme contingency referred to in sub-clause 9.4 [and the Employer shall be released from all liability to the Contractor in connection with the matter].

10.3.3 If the cause of the claim has a continuing effect, the Contractor shall update the information at monthly intervals

(1) stating the extension of time and adjustment to the Contract Sum claimed for delay and cost already incurred and

(2) so far as practicable, proposing a final adjustment to the Contract Sum and Date for Substantial Completion of the Works and any affected Section and

(3) providing any other information the Employer's Representative reasonably requires.

10.3.4 The Contractor shall keep detailed contemporary records to substantiate any aspect of an vent or circumstance about which it has given, or is entitled to give, notice under this sub-clause 10.3, and its resulting costs. These shall include any records the Employer's Representative directs the Contractor to keep. The Contractor shall give the records to the Employer's Representative if so directed.

Note

There are 13 Compensation Events listed in the Schedule, Part 1, Section K, with a further four (numbers 18–21) under certain circumstances, are electable by the Employer. Should a Compensation Event arise, then before the Contract Sum is adjusted by the Employer's Representative the following criteria must be satisfied:

(i) The Compensation Event is not a result of an act or omission of the Contractor or Contractor's Personnel, or the Contractor's breach of the Contract;

(ii) The Contractor cannot avoid the adverse effects of the Compensation Event and makes all reasonable efforts to minimise them;

(iii) The Contractor has complied with this clause 10 in full (including giving notices and details within the time required);

(iv) The Contract does not provide otherwise;

(v) For items 10, 18, 19, 20 and 21 of the Schedule, Section K, the delay events must be unforeseeable.

The second criteria—that the Contractor cannot avoid the adverse effects of the Compensation Event and makes all reasonable efforts to minimise them—could be construed by the Employer's Representative as an obligation on the Contractor to accelerate or revise the programme for the Works in order to reduce or eradicate the delay.

If the Contractor considers that there should be an extension of time or an adjustment to the Contract Sum, or if any other entitlement exists, he shall provide such notice to the Employer's Representative within 20 working days after he becomes aware, or should have been aware of something that would give rise to an entitlement. The notice must comply with Condition 4.14 (Communications) and be sent to the person identified in the Schedule, Part 1, Section A. The notice must prominently state that it is being given under sub-clause 10.3.

Sub-Clause 4.10.2 (10) requires the Contractor to include in its progress reports details of anything that might have an adverse effect on the execution of the Works, the steps the Contractor is taking or proposes to take to reduce those risks and any steps that the Contractor proposes that the Employer or the Employer's Personnel take to reduce those risks. The Contractor should include a list of all sub-clause 10.3 notices within the progress reports.

Within a further 20 working days the Contractor shall provide:

(i) All relevant facts;

(ii) A detailed calculation and a proposal based on the calculation of the adjustment to be made to the Contract Sum and of the amount of any other entitlement claimed by the Contractor;

(iii) Details of the amount of the contingency referred to in sub-clause 9.4 to be used, or details of the effect on programme and completion dates.

The Employer's Representative may request the Contractor to provide further information.

If the Contractor does not comply with notices, details and time scales set down in sub-clause 10.3 then the Contractor shall not be entitled to an increase in the Contract Sum or an extension of time or use of the programme contingency referred to in sub-clause 9.4 and the Employer shall be released from all liability to the Contractor in relation to the matter.

Contractors must comply with all the requirements of the Contract as set down in Conditions 9 and 10 if they are to avail of entitlements in relation to extensions of time, Compensation Events and adjustments to the Contract. This places obligations on Contractors to maintain records and issue notices in strict compliance with the Contract, otherwise entitlements may be forfeited. The Contractor's obligations are further set out in Condition 10.3.4.

If the cause of the claim has a continuing effect the Contractor shall update all the information at monthly intervals. The Contractor will have to:

(i) State the extension of time and adjustment to the Contract Sum claimed in respect of any delay and cost already incurred;
(ii) Propose a final adjustment to the Contract Sum and the Date for Substantial Completion of the Works and any affected section;
(iii) Provide any other information that the Employer's Representative requires.

Sub-clause 10.3.4 requires the Contractor to keep contemporary records of all events under clause 10.3. The Employer's Representative may instruct the Contractor to keep such records.

The importance of compliance with the stated timescales for the service of notices and documents cannot be overstated. Recent case law in the Britain and Northern Ireland have held that where there are clear contractual terms as to claim procedures, then the courts are not favourable to the party that fails to comply with the contract claims procedures. Claim notices for entitlements should be clearly drafted, be unambiguous, notify the event and state the contract clause under which the notice is served.

10.4 Proposed Instructions

The Employer's Representative may direct the Contractor to make proposals for a proposed instruction. The Contractor shall not implement the proposed instruction unless and until the Employer's Representative has confirmed the instruction as given. Within 20 working days after the Employer's Representative directs the Contractor to make proposals, the Contractor shall give to the Employer's Representative all of the following:

(1) a detailed calculation and proposal, based on the calculation, of any adjustment to the Contract Sum that would result from the proposed instruction

(2) if the proposed instruction would cause a delay, the information required under sub-clause 9.3, and a proposal, based on that information for any use of the programme contingency referred to in sub-clause 9.4 or extension to the Date for Substantial Completion of the Works and any affected Section

(3) if the proposed instruction is to omit any of the Works, a revised programme and, if appropriate, a proposed earlier Date for Substantial Completion of the Works and any affected Section

(4) any Contractor's Documents required in connection with the proposed instruction, or a timetable for them.

Note
The Employer's Representative may request the Contractor to provide a proposal on a proposed instruction. The Contractor has 20 working days to provide the details, which will include:

(i) Calculation of the adjustment to the Contract Sum;

(ii) Details of any delay and information required under clause 9.3 with regards to the Date for Substantial Completion of the Works or any section of the Works;
(iii) A revised programme in the case of an omission, and, if appropriate, a proposed earlier Date for Substantial Completion;
(iv) Contractor's Documents required in relation to the proposal or a timetable for them.

The Contractor shall not implement the proposed instruction until the Employer's Representative confirms the instruction as given.

10.5 Employer's Representative's Determination

10.5.1 If the Contractor has made a claim or proposal under sub-clauses 10.3 or 10.4, the Employer's Representative shall, within 20 working days of receiving it, do one of the following:
(1) direct the Contractor to give additional information or revised proposals, in which case the Contractor shall do so within 10 working days and the Employer's Representative shall reply in accordance with this sub-clause within a further 10 working days, but that reply must not require the Contractor to give additional information or a revised proposal
(2) notify the Contractor and the Employer that the Contractor's proposals are agreed and make any resulting adjustments to the Contract Sum, use of the programme contingency referred to in sub-clause 9.4 or extension to the Date for Substantial Completion of the Works and any affected Section
(3) make a determination of any adjustments to the Contract Sum, use of the programme contingency referred to in sub-clause 9.4 or extension to the Date for Substantial Completion of the Works and any affected Section, and notify the Contractor and the Employer
(4) in response to a proposal under sub-clause 10.4, notify the Contractor that the proposed instruction will not be given.

10.5.2 The Employer's Representative may [but is not bound to] determine an extension of time for a Compensation Event that is a breach of the Contract by the Employer on its own initiative even if the Contractor has not made a claim or proposal under sub-clauses 10.3 or 10.4.

Note

The Employer's Representative has 20 working days to respond to a Contractor's claim under sub-clause 10.3 or a proposal under sub-clause 10.4. He may:

(i) Request more information or a revised proposal—the Contractor then has 10 working to respond. The Employer's Representative then has a further 10 working days to reply;
(ii) Notify the Employer and the Contractor that the Contractor's proposals are agreed and make any resulting adjustment to the Contract Sum, use of the programme contingency referred to in sub-clause 9.4, or extension to the date of Substantial Completion of the Works and any affected section;
(iii) Make a determination of the adjustment to the Contract Sum, use of the programme contingency referred to in sub-clause 9.4, or extension to the date of Substantial Completion of the Works and any affected section, and notify the Contractor and the Employer;
(iv) In response to a Contractor's proposal issued under sub-clause 10.4, notify the Contractor that the proposed instruction will not be given.

Where the Contractor has not made a claim under sub-clause 10.3 or submitted a proposal under sub-clause 10.4, the Employer's Representative may work (but is not bound to) on his own initiative in making an adjustment to the Contract Sum or extending the Date for Substantial Completion of the Works.

10.5.3 If the Employer's Representative fails to take any of the actions in sub-clause 10.5.1 within the time stated, the Employer's Representative will be taken to have made a determination under sub-clause 10.5.1(3) that there be no adjustment to the Contract Sum, no use of programme contingency referred to in sub-clause 9.4, and no extension to any Date for Substantial Completion. The determination will be taken to have been made on the last day of the time provided for in sub-clause 10.5.1.

Note
The Contractor should carefully note that if the Employer's Representative fails to take action under Condition 10.5.1 within the time stated, this indicates his decision that there was no adjustment of any description to the Contract Sum.

10.5.4 A determination of the Employer's Representative notified to the Contractor and the Employer under sub-clause 10.5.1(3) or 10.5.2 shall be final and binding on the Parties unless, within 28 days after receiving notice of the determination (or, if sub-clause 10.5.3 applies, within 28 days after the determination is taken to have been made), the Contractor or the Employer gives notice to the other under sub-clause 13.1.1 or under sub-clause 13.2.1 disputing the determination and referring the dispute to either;

1. the dispute management procedure under sub-clause 13.1; or
2. conciliation under sub-clause 13.2

Note
Should the Contractor fail to give notice within the specified time of 28 days from the receipt of the notice of determination, the Contractor no longer has any entitlement as the determination of the Employer's Representative becomes final and binding.

10.5.5 Notice of an agreement under sub-clause 10.5.1(2) shall be final and binding on the Parties unless, within 28 days after receiving the notice, either:

(1) the Contractor both (a) notifies the Employer's Representative and the Employer that the Contractor disagrees that the notice correctly records agreed terms and (b) gives notice to the Employer under sub-clause 13.1.1 or under sub-clause 13.2.1referring the dispute to either;

1. the dispute management procedure under sub-clause 13.1; or
2. conciliation under sub-clause 13.2.

or

(2) the Employer both (a) notifies the Employer's Representative and the Contractor that the Employer does not agree with the terms notified by the Employer's Representative and (b) gives notice to the Contractor under sub-clause 13.1.1 or under sub-clause 12.1.1 referring the dispute to either;

1. the dispute management procedure under sub-clause 13.1; or
2. conciliation under sub-clause 13.2

Note
Either Party may dispute the determination of the Employer's Representative, provided the notice to the specified timescale

10.6 Adjustments to the Contract Sum

Adjustments to the Contract Sum for a Compensation Event shall only be for the value of any additional, substituted, and omitted work required as a result of the Compensation Event under this sub-clause 10.6 and any delay cost under sub-clause 10.7. [Where an adjustment to the Contract Sum arises from additional, substituted or omitted named Specialists' Works, the percentage addition tendered by the Contractor for that named Specialist, and included in the Schedule Part 3B, shall be taken into account in the valuation]. Additional, substituted, and omitted work shall be valued as follows:

10.6.1 If the Compensation Event requires additional, substituted or omitted work, similar to work for which there are rates in the Pricing Document, to be executed under similar conditions, the determination shall use those rates.

10.6.2 If the Compensation Event requires additional, substituted or omitted work that is not similar to work for which there are rates in the Pricing Document, or is not to be executed under similar conditions, the determination shall be on the basis of the rates in the Pricing Document when that is reasonable.

10.6.3 If the adjustment cannot be determined under the above rules, the Employer's Representative shall make a fair valuation based on rates for similar work in the locality, if available.

10.6.4 Instead of sub-clauses 10.6.1, 10.6.2 and 10.6.3 applying, the Employer's Representative may conclusively direct that additional or substituted work required as a result of a Compensation Event be determined (in full or in part) on the basis of the cost of performing the additional or substituted work, compared with the Contractor's cost without the Compensation Event, determined as follows: [Where the additional or substituted work includes named Specialists' Works, the determined value shall be based on the tendered hourly rates, the tendered percentage addition for costs of materials and the tendered percentage addition/deduction for costs of plant as tendered by the respective named Specialist.]

(1) the number of hours worked or to be worked by each category of work person stated in the Schedule, part 2D, and engaged on the work to which the Compensation Event relates, on or off the Site, multiplied in each case by the tendered hourly rate for that category stated in the Schedule, part 2D (But if any of the tendered hourly rates are less than 75% of the relevant rate (in the case of Craftspersons this means 75% of the Craftsman's rate, or in the case of General Operatives, 75% x 88% of the Craftsman's rate, or in the case of Apprentices, 75% x 62% of the Craftsman's rate) in the construction industry registered employment agreement current on the Designated Date, they will be read instead as 75% of the relevant rate in that agreement (in the case of Craftspersons this means 75% of the Craftsman's rate, in the case of General Operatives, 75% x 88% of the Craftsman's rate, in the case of Apprentices, 75% x 62% of the Craftsman's rate)) and

(2) the cost of materials used in that work, taking into account discounts and excluding VAT, plus the percentage adjustment tendered by the Contractor and stated in the Schedule, part 2D (But if the percentage adjustment tendered is negative or blank it will be read as 0%) and

(3) the cost of plant reasonably used for that work, whether hired or owned by the Contractor, at the rates in the document listed in the Schedule, part 1K (as that document may be modified according to the Schedule, part 1K) plus or minus the percentage adjustment tendered by the Contractor and included in the Schedule, part 2D (But if the percentage adjustment tendered is a deduction of more than 100% it will be read as a deduction of 100% or if the entry is blank it will be read as 0%). If the document listed in the Schedule does not give a rate for a plant item, a market rental rate shall be used, plus or minus the percentage adjustment.

Note

The adjustment to the Contract Sum for a Compensation Event is carried out by using rates contained in the Pricing Document, fair rates or recorded hours by the rates stated in the Schedule, Part 2E, together with the cost of plant and materials with the percentage additions quoted in the Schedule, Part 2E.

The Employer's Representative may direct that additional or substituted Works required as a result of a Compensation Event be determined in accordance with the Contractor's tendered hourly labour rates and the Contractor's tendered percentage addition to the cost of plant and materials.

At the time of writing, the first Sectoral Employment Order for the construction industry is under preparation. When introduced it is expected that Condition 10.6.4 (3) will be amended.

10.7 Delay Cost

10.7.1 If the Date for Substantial Completion of the Works has been extended because of a Compensation Event [and not otherwise, and subject to sub-clause 10.7.2], there shall be added to the Contract Sum an amount for delay cost, either (whichever it says in the Schedule, part 1K)

(1) for each Site Working Day for which the Date for Substantial Completion of the Works has been extended because of the Compensation Event, the daily rate of delay cost tendered by the Contractor in the Schedule, part 2D [and to the extent that named Specialists' Works are delayed by a Compensation Event under the Contract between the Employer and Contractor, the tendered rate of delay costs for the respective named Specialists shall be used to determine the delay cost]

or

(2) the expenses [excluding profit and loss of profit] unavoidably incurred by the Contractor as a result of the delay to the Date for Substantial Completion of the Works caused by the Compensation Event in respect of which that date has been extended under the Contract.

10.7.2 If the Works are concurrently delayed by more than one cause, and one or more of the causes is not a Compensation Event, there shall be no increase to the Contract Sum for delay cost for the period of concurrent delay.

Note

Sub-Clause 10.7.1(1) takes into account the introduction of the procedures for Named Specialist Work.

Sub-clause 10.7.2 provides that if a delay has more than one cause, and one or more of the causes is not a Compensation Event, there shall be no increase to the Contract Sum for delay costs for the period of concurrent delay. This removes any dispute or ambiguity about which delay is the dominant delay and whether compensation is due to the Contractor as a result of the dominant delay.

10.7.3 If, as a result of a Compensation Event, the Date for Substantial Completion of the Works has been extended, so that there is a period of 7 or more consecutive non-working days in the time between the Starting Date and the Date for Substantial Completion of the Works, and that would not have occurred without the Compensation Event happening, then the Contractor's expenses [excluding profit and loss of profit] unavoidably incurred because of this delay shall be included in the determination of the addition to the Contract Sum for delay cost. But the amount so added shall not exceed the amount stated in the Schedule, part 2D, as the Contractor's tendered rate of delay cost multiplied by the number of additional non- working days, if there is an amount stated there. **Non-working day** means a day that, for good reason, is not a Site Working Day [such as a trade holiday].

Note

Sub-Clause 1.2.2 (11) describes a working day as a day that is not Saturday, Sunday, a public holiday established under the Organisation of Working Time Act or Good Friday.

10.7.4 Except as provided in this sub-clause 10.7 [notwithstanding anything else in the Contract] losses or expenses arising from or in connection with delay, disruption, acceleration, loss of productivity or knock-on effect shall not be taken into account or included in any increase to the Contract Sum, and the Employer shall have no liability for such losses or expenses.

10.7.5 [There shall be no delay cost paid as a result of extensions to the Date for Substantial Completion of a Section].

10.7.6 If the Schedule states more than one rate for delay cost, the rate for the period when the delay occurred or delayed part of the Works shall be used. This shall be determined by the Employer's Representative.

Note
Delay costs are added as defined in the Schedule, Part 2 E. The Contractor's delay costs are capped to that stated in the Schedule. Sub-clause 10.7.2 provides for holiday(s) within an extended period to payment for costs incurred, but the costs are capped at the daily delay cost tendered rate stated in the Schedule, Part 2E.

Losses or expenses arising from or in relation to delay, disruption, loss of productivity or knock-on effect shall not be taken into account or included in any assessment of an increase to the Contract Sum. The Employer has no liability for such losses or expenses.

There will be no delay costs paid as a result of extensions to the Date for Substantial Completion of a Section.

10.8 Price Variation

The Contract includes clause PV1 or clause PV2, whichever is stated in the Schedule, part 1M.

Note
Sub-clause 10.8 deals with price variation. There are two approaches electable at the discretion of the Employer in the Schedule, Part 1:

(i) The Proven Cost Method (PV1);
This is an invoice-based system whereby the Contractor establishes his entitlement after the fixed-price period by invoices which are checked by the Employer. The definition of Base Date under PV1 is the first day of the thirty-first month after the Contract date, so that this approach guarantees the Employer the 30-month fixed price even if there should be a delay in setting the Contract Date.

(ii) The Formula Fluctuations Method (PV2);
This is based on the use of CSO Indices for different categories of materials, fuels and CPI, as published in the Wholesale Price Indices. The weighting for each of the materials, fuel, labour, non-reusable temporary works and non-recoverable overheads are established by the Employer and the proportions of different fuels and materials are also defined for use with these indices, and these proportions are provided in the Invitation to Tender.

10.9 Employer's Claims

10.9.1 If the Employer or the Employer's Representative considers that, under the Contract, there should be a reduction of the Contract Sum, or that any amount is due to the Employer from the Contractor under the Contract, the Employer or the Employer's Representative shall, as soon as practicable, give notice and particulars of the event or circumstances to the other, and to the Contractor. The notice shall include

(1) details of the event or circumstances giving rise to the notice, and all relevant facts and

(2) a calculation, and a proposal based on that calculation, of any adjustment to be made to the Contract Sum or any amount due by the Contractor to the Employer.

10.9.2 The Contractor shall be entitled, within 20 working days of receipt of such a notice, to give a response to the Employer's Representative and shall, if the notice was given by the Employer, give a copy of any response to the Employer. Within 20 working days after receiving the Contractor's response, or after the time for responding has elapsed, if the Contractor has not responded within that time, the Employer's Representative shall determine the matter in accordance with the Contract.

10.9.3 The Employer may deduct from any amount due to the Contractor

(1) any amount determined by the Employer's Representative to be due, or likely to become due, from the Contractor to the Employer under the Contract and

(2) any amount due from the Contractor to the Employer under any contract.

10.9.4 The procedure in this sub-clause 10.9 shall apply until either the Defects Certificate or the certificates required following termination have been issued, but this does not limit the Employer's rights after then.

Note

The Contractor can be liable to the Employer for any monies the Employer or the Employer's Representative may consider due to the Employer. The Contractor shall pay these monies to the Employer, or the Employer may deduct the money from payments on the particular project or any other contract.

The Employer's claims are not time-barred as the Contractors are under sub-clause 10.3. The Contractor has 20 working days to respond to such a notice to the Employer's Representative and the Employer (if the notice was sent by the Employer). The Employer Representative has 20 working days to consider the matter.

Notice of the event and a calculation of the adjustment to the Contract Sum must be provided to the Contractor by either the Employer or the Employer's Representative before any adjustments can be made to the Contract Sum.

General Notes on Clause 10

This clause deals with the manner in which both Delay Events and compensation costs will be evaluated. This is an innovative approach to the management of claims, requiring strict adherence to procedures in order to preserve an entitlement to claim.

Every single event in respect of which compensation is to be claimed must be processed under sub-clause 10.3. The amount of detail required is substantial and where the claim arises, for example, from an instructed variation, the requirement and responsibility to furnish the notice and the documentation rests with the Contractor. Notices, within the specified time periods, must be submitted in order to preserve entitlements.

Schedule 1, Section K, is central to the Contract, as the lists contained in the Schedule set out when compensation will be payable and when extensions of time can be granted. If the event does not appear on the list in the Schedule no compensation will be payable nor will extensions to the Date for Substantial Completion be made.

Sub-clause 10.4 provides that, prior to issuing an instruction, the Employer's Representative can instruct the Contractor to prepare an assessment, in terms of time and money, of a proposed instruction. The Contractor should note the additional burden placed upon him in the preparation of documents and programmes for a Work Item that may not proceed. There is no provision for the Employer to compensate the Contractor for any administration work or associated costs.

In practical terms this is a Fixed Price Lump Sum Contract which does not allow for price variation in any meaningful way except for increases in PRSI, VAT and excise duties which can be reimbursed at costs.

11 PAYMENT

11.1 Interim Payment

11.1.1 At each of the following times
- (i) the periods for interim payment stated in the Schedule, part 1L, if the amount payable is more than the minimum amount stated in the Schedule and
- (ii) upon issue of the certificate of Substantial Completion for the Works or any Section

the Contractor shall give a payment claim notice to the Employer's Representative, in the form of an interim statement, [not later than 5 days after the date agreed between the Parties to be the payment claim date], showing all of the following:
- (1) the progress of the Works
- (2) the instalment of the Contract Sum that the Contractor considers should, under the Contract, be paid on an interim basis
- (3) a detailed breakdown using the Pricing Document, and individually detailing proposed payments to named Specialists so that payments to each named Specialists are easily distinguished from each other.
- (4) any supporting evidence the Employer's Representative requires.

The interim statement given on Substantial Completion shall include all amounts due to the Contractor at that time for the Works or Section.

11.1.2 The instalment of the Contract Sum that the Contractor shall be entitled to be paid on an interim basis shall be
- (1) the Contract value of the Works properly executed by the Contractor [according to the Pricing Document, as a portion of the Contract Sum] and
- (2) any amount the Employer's Representative considers proper under sub-clause 11.2 and
- (3) amounts for adjustments to the Contract Sum for Compensation Events, as determined under the Contract and
- (4) any amount to be paid according to clause PV1 or PV2, whichever is part of the Contract and
- (5) amounts included in the Pricing Document for Contractor's Documents properly completed and supplied as required by the Contract.

11.1.3 Within 14 days of receipt of the payment claim notice the Employer's Representative shall issue a response to the payment claim notice to the Contractor in the form of a certificate, sending a copy to the Employer, setting out the amount of interim payment that, in the Employer's Representative's opinion, is to be made by the Employer to the Contractor, taking account of retention under sub-clause 11.3 and deductions and amounts due from the Contractor to the Employer [including damages for delay and deductions under sub-clause 11.4], together with calculations and the reasons for the opinion. The Employer's Representative shall issue to the individual named Specialists, details of the gross and net amount included within the certificate to the respective named Specialists.

11.1.4 If there is a sum due to the Contractor, the Contractor shall send an invoice to the Employer for that sum after receiving the response to the payment claim notice. The Employer shall pay the amount due on the invoice within 21 days after receiving the invoice.

Note

This Condition contains the necessary amendments to comply with the Construction Contracts Act 2013. The time of Interim Payments will be stated in Part 1L of the Schedule. At the time for an Interim Payment the Contractor shall provide to the Employer's Representative a statement showing:

- (i) The progress of the Works;
- (ii) The instalment that the Contractor should be paid;

(iii) A detailed breakdown;
(iv) Any supporting details the Employer's Representative requires;
(v) Not stated in sub-clause 11.1.2 but contained in sub-clause 5.3.7, the Contractor must supply with each Interim Statement a Certificate stating that the Contractor has complied in full with sub-clause 5.3 (Pay and Conditions of Employment); see sub-clause 11.4.4 for the severe effect of non-compliance with sub-clause 5.3.7.

Within 10 days of receipt of the Contractor's Interim Statement the Employer's Representative shall issue a Certificate setting out the amounts due to the Contractor (if any) after taking account of any amount due from the Contractor to the Employer and charges referred to in sub-clause 7.12. The Employer's Representative has to provide the calculations and reasons for his opinion in support of the Certificate.

The Contractor has to provide an invoice to the Employer for any amount due to him as directed by the Payment Certificate. The Employer then pays the amount within 21 days after receipt of the invoice.

Note: Allowance has to be made for weekends, public holidays, annual industry holidays and any other non-working day specified in the Contract.

11.2 Unfixed Works Items

At the discretion of the Employer's Representative, but only when so provided in the Schedule, part 1L, interim payments may include any amount, not exceeding the percentage of value stated in the Schedule, part 1L, the Employer's Representative considers proper for each of the following:

(1) the Contract value of any Works Items that comply with all of the following requirements, all to the satisfaction of the Employer's Representative:
  (a) they have been completed and are substantially ready to be incorporated in the Works
  (b) title to them has been vested in the Employer
  (c) they are stored suitably at the Site
  (d) they have not been delivered to the Site prematurely

(2) the Contract value of any Work Items not delivered to the Site that comply with all of the following requirements, all to the satisfaction of the Employer's Representative:
  (a) they have been completed and are substantially ready to be incorporated in the Works
  (b) title to them has been vested in the Employer
  (c) they are stored suitably and set aside and marked to show clearly that their destination is the Site and that they are the property of the Employer
  (d) they are clearly identified in a list given to the Employer's Representative, together with documentary evidence that title is vested in the Employer
  (e) they are insured as required by the Contract, and will be insured as required while in transit
  (f) the Contractor has given the Employer a bond in the form for such bonds in the Works Requirements, or if there is none, a form approved by the Employer, executed by a surety approved by the Employer's Representative, for the amount to be paid.

In this clause 11.2, the Contract value of a Works Item means a portion of the Contract Sum the Employer's Representative determines is for supplying of the Works Item, having regard to the Pricing Document. [If the Pricing Document has a rate or price for supplying and fixing a Works Item, the Contract value includes only the portion for supplying the Works Item, as determined by the Employer's Representative.]

Note
The Contractor can be paid for unfixed Works Items up to the value as detailed in Part 1 L of the Schedule, provided

(i) They have been completed and they are substantially ready to be incorporated into the Works;
(ii) Title to them has been vested in the Employer;
(iii) They are stored suitably on site;
(iv) They have not been brought to the site prematurely.

Payment for unfixed Work Items is at the discretion of the Employer's Representative.

Payment for goods not delivered to the site is governed by the following:

(i) They have been completed and are substantially ready to be incorporated in the Works;
(ii) Title to them has been vested in the Employer;
(iii) They are stored suitably and marked to show that they are the property of the Employer and that their destination is the site;
(iv) They are clearly identified in a list provided to the Employer's Representative and with documentary evidence that title is vested in the Employer;
(v) They are insured as required by the Contract and will be insured while in transit;
(vi) The Employer is provided with a bond by a surety approved by the Employer's Representative for the amount to be paid.

11.3 Retention

11.3.1 There shall be deducted from each interim payment to the Contractor the retention percentage stated in the Schedule, part 1L.

11.3.2 Upon issue of the certificate of Substantial Completion of the Works, the Contractor shall be entitled to invoice the Employer for half of the amount so retained and the Contractor shall furnish the Employer's Representative with a copy of the invoice. Upon the issue of the Defects Certificate, the Contractor shall be entitled to invoice the Employer for the balance of the money so retained and the Contractor shall furnish the Employer's Representative with a copy of the invoice.

11.3.3 If, within 14 days of the issue of the certificate of Substantial Completion of the Works, or another date agreed by the Employer's Representative, the Contractor provides to the Employer a retention bond in the form in the Work Requirements, or, if there is none, a form approved by the Employer, for the amount retained by the Employer, and executed by a surety approved by the Employer, the Contractor shall be entitled to invoice the Employer for the balance of the money retained.

11.3.4 Upon issue of the certificate of Substantial Completion of a Section of the Works, the retention amount to be withheld until issue of the certificate of Substantial Completion of the Works shall be reduced by the amount stated in the Schedule, part 1G, and the Contractor shall be entitled to invoice the Employer for that amount.

11.3.5 The Employer shall pay the Contractor the amount due on an invoice under this sub-clause 11.3 within 21 days after receiving the invoice [less any amount that the Employer is entitled to deduct according to sub-clause 10.9].

11.4 Full Payment

The payments to the Contractor under this Contract are for compliance in full with the Contractor's obligations to the time of payment [including construction management, programming, reporting, payment of wages and observing employment requirements] [but payment does not imply acceptance that the obligations have been performed]. When the Contractor has not fully complied with its obligations, the Employer is not required to make payment in full [without limiting its other rights or remedies]. In particular

11.4.1 If the Contractor has not given a collateral warranty by the date stated in the Schedule, part 1F(i), the Employer is entitled to deduct from payment to the Contractor the amount stated in the Schedule, part 1F(i) until the collateral warranty is given.

11.4.2 If the Contractor has not submitted a programme or given a progress report when required by sub-clauses 4.9 and 4.10, the Employer is entitled to deduct 15% of each payment to the Contractor until the programme or report has been submitted or given.

11.4.3 If the Contractor has not complied with sub-clause 5.3, the Employer is entitled to make the deduction provided for in sub-clause 5.3.6.

11.4.4 If the Contractor does not give the certificate required by sub-clause 5.3.7 with an interim statement, there shall be no payment due under sub-clause 11.1 for the relevant Work Item until the certificate is given.

11.4.5 Deductions from payments because of obligations that the Contractor has still not complied with by the date the Defects Certificate was issued shall be deducted from the Contract Sum. In the case of a deduction from the Contract Sum because of failure to give the certificate required by sub-clause 5.3.7, the amount deducted shall be the portion of the Contract value of the relevant Work Item that the Employer determines to be the labour portion. The Contractor shall give the Employer any information the Employer requires for this determination.

Note

Full payment is dependent on:

(i) The Contractor has providing all the collateral warranties, otherwise the Employer may deduct the amount stated in Part1F of the Schedule;

(ii) The Contractor submitting a programme or a revised programme or progress report otherwise the Employer may deduct 15% of each payment until the programme and/or reports are submitted;

(iii) The Contractor complying with sub-clause 5.3 (Pay and Conditions of Employment), otherwise the Employer may make the deduction provided for in sub-clause 5.3.6;

(iv) The Contractor providing a Certificate as required by sub-clause 5.3.7, otherwise there shall be no payment due for the relevant Work Item until the Certificate is submitted or provided;

(v) The Contractor complying with all his obligations by the date the Defects Certificate is issued.

If there is any deduction to the Contract Sum as a result of the Contractor's failure to provide the Certificate required by sub-clause 5.3.7, the amount deducted shall be the labour-element value for the portion of Works, as determined by the Employer. The Contractor has to provide the Employer with any information the Employer requires in order to make the determination.

11.5 Final Statement

11.5.1 Within 2 months after Substantial Completion of the Works is certified, the Contractor shall give to the Employer's Representative a final statement. The Contractor shall include in that statement all money that the Contractor considers to be due from the Employer to the Contractor under or in connection with the Contract. The Employer shall have no liability to the Contractor under or in connection with the Contract for any matter not detailed in the final statement, except under the indemnities in the Contract or Compensation Events occurring after Substantial Completion of the Works was certified. If no final statement is given within the time required, the Employer shall be released from all liability to the Contractor under or in connection with the Contract.

11.5.2 Within 3 months after receipt of the Contractor's final statement, the Employer's Representative shall issue to the Contractor and to the Employer a penultimate payment certificate certifying the amount that, in the Employer's Representative's opinion, will be due from the Employer to the Contractor, less any final retention to be paid after the Defects Certificate is issued, or from the Contractor to the Employer.

11.5.3 As soon as practicable, no more than 3 months, after the Defects Certificate is issued, the Employer's Representative shall issue a final payment certificate certifying the amount that, in the Employer's Representative's opinion, is finally due from the Employer to the Contractor, or from the Contractor to the Employer. The amount in the final payment certificate shall be the same as the amount in the penultimate payment certificate, except for

(1) the final payment of retention and
(2) adjustments to the Contract Sum because of Compensation Events that happen after Substantial Completion of the Works is certified and
(3) amounts owed by the Contractor that were not included in the penultimate certificate [for example, for Defects that the Contractor has not rectified] and
(4) deductions from the Contract Sum under sub-clause 11.4 and
(5) other amounts that, according to the Contract, are to be paid after Substantial Completion of the Works [such as payments for testing after Substantial Completion].

11.5.4 If the penultimate or final payment certificate states that there is a sum owing to the Contractor, the Contractor shall issue an invoice to the Employer for that sum and the Employer shall pay the amount due on the invoice within 21 days after receiving the invoice. If the penultimate or final payment certificate states that there is a sum owing to the Employer, the Contractor shall pay the amount due within 14 days of receipt of the Employer's demand for payment. [Payments and certificates, including the penultimate and final payment certificates and the Defects Certificate, will not relieve the Contractor of any obligations, or be evidence of the value of work or that work has been completed satisfactorily].

Note

Within 2 months after Substantial Completion, the Contractor shall provide a Final Statement which shall include all money that the Contractor considers due from the Employer. The Employer shall have no liability to the Contractor for any matter not detailed in the Final Statement except for indemnities or Compensation Events occurring after Substantial Completion. The time for the preparation and submission of the Final Statement is very short. This means the Contractor will have to compile the Final Account as the Works are ongoing. The Contractor must ensure that subcontractors also provide details of their accounts diligently to the Contractor for incorporation into the Final Statement.

The Contractor's Final Statement must be a comprehensive document that includes all items that the Contractor claims payment for.

The Final Certificate cannot adjust any value(s) contained in the Penultimate Certificate. Similarly items for which the Contractor claims payment that were not included in his Final Statement cannot be included in the Final Certificate. The onus is on the Contractor to ensure that his Final Statement is a comprehensive document.

Monies to be paid to the Contractor as detailed in the Penultimate or Final Certificate shall become due and be paid by the Employer within 15 working days after receipt by the Employer of the Contractor's invoice.

Monies to be paid by the Contractor to the Employer as detailed in the Penultimate or Final Certificate shall be paid by the Contractor within 10 working days of receipt of the Employer's demand.

Payments and Certificates (Interim Payment Certificates, Penultimate Certificates, Final Certificate and Defects Certificates) will not be evidence that the Works have been carried out satisfactorily or relieve the Contractor of any of his contractual obligations.

Late payments attract interest at the rate provided in the European Communities (Late Payment in Commercial Transactions) Regulations 2012.

11.6 Time for Payment and Interest

11.6.1 When a payment is to be made under the Contract, and no time for payment is stated, the amount due shall be paid within 30 days of receipt of a demand for payment.

11.6.2 Interest shall be added to any payment not made within the time provided in the Contract, from the date the payment was due under the Contract, at the rate provided in the European Communities (Late Payment in Commercial Transactions) Regulations 2012.

11.7 Value Added Tax

11.7.1 The Contractor's completed form of tender states whether, and to what extent, the Contract Sum includes VAT.

11.7.2 To the extent that the Contract Sum excludes VAT, the Employer shall pay the Contractor (or the Revenue Commissioners when required by Law or their practice) any VAT arising on the supply under the Contract in addition to the Contract Sum.

11.7.3 To the extent that the Contract Sum includes VAT,

(1) adjustments to the Contract Sum shall be on a net-of-Vat basis, and the appropriate sum for VAT shall be added or subtracted and

(2) any VAT included in the Contract Sum that the Employer is required to pay the Revenue Commissioners (by Law or their practice) shall be deducted from the Contract Sum.

11.7.4 So therefore, if the Contract Sum includes VAT chargeable at the standard rate only, then the Employer shall pay the Contractor (or the Revenue Commissioners when required by Law or their practice).

- The Contract Sum, including the VAT chargeable at the standard rate that is included in the Contract Sum and also
- Any VAT arising on the supply under the Contract that is chargeable at another rate.

In the Contract 'standard rate' means the VAT rate specified in section 46(1)(a) of the Value-Added Tax Consolidation Act, 2010.

11.7.5 Amounts in the Contract other than the Contract Sum exclude VAT, unless otherwise stated.

11.7.6 The Contractor shall send the Employer, for each payment, an invoice complying with 66 of the Value-Added Tax Consolidation Act, 2010.

11.8 Withholding Tax

The Employer shall be entitled to make any deduction or withholding on account of tax required by Legal Requirements or the practice of the Revenue Commissioners.

12 TERMINATION

12.1 Termination on Contractor Default

12.1.1 The Employer may, without limiting any other right or remedy, terminate the Contractor's obligation to complete the Works by notice to the Contractor if any of the following occurs:

(1) the Contractor fails to comply with its obligations under the Contract, and, if the failure can be cured, the Employer's Representative has directed the Contractor to put the matter right, and the Contractor has not done so within 14 days after receiving the direction

(2) the Contractor abandons or, except where required or permitted by the Contract, suspends the execution of the Works

(3) the Contractor fails to proceed regularly and diligently with the execution of the Works

(4) the Contractor fails to maintain the required insurances or performance bond

(5) the Starting Date has not occurred or the Contractor has not started to execute the Works on the Site within 6 weeks of the date the Contract requires

(6) any of the Contractor's warranties in sub-clause 2.5 or sub-clause 2.6 are untrue

(7) the Contractor has committed or caused the Employer to commit a serious breach of Legal Requirements concerning the Works

(8) the Contractor or Contractor's Personnel have committed a breach of the Safety, Health and Welfare at Work Act 2005 or any regulations or code of practice made under it concerning the Works

(9) the Contractor has not complied with sub-clauses 5.3.2 or 5.3.3 either (a) within 14 days after notice from the Employer requiring a failure to be put right or (b) persistently

(10) the Contractor has subcontracted all or any part of the Works in breach of the Contract

(11) any of the following **insolvency events** occur:

  (a) a petition is presented to wind up the Contractor and is not dismissed within 10 working days of presentation

  (b) any meeting of creditors or members of the Contractor is convened or held for the purpose of considering a resolution to wind up the Contractor

  (c) any arrangement or composition with or for the benefit of its creditors [including any compromises or arrangements entered into under sections 201 to 204 of the Companies Act 1963] are proposed or entered into by or in respect of the Contractor

  (d) a liquidator, supervisor, receiver, administrator, administrative receiver, trustee or encumbrancer takes possession of or is appointed over the Contractor or any of its assets, or any distress, execution or other process is levied or enforced, and not discharged within 10 working days, on the Contractor or any of its assets

  (e) the Contractor ceases or threatens to cease carrying on business, or is, or is regarded by law or by a court to be, or declares itself to be, insolvent or unable to pay its debts as they fall due

  (f) a petition is presented to appoint an examiner to the Contractor, or an order is made appointing an examiner to the Contractor

  (g) the Contractor, being an individual, becomes bankrupt

  (h) any event similar to the above insolvency events occurs in respect of the Contractor in any jurisdiction in which it is incorporated or has a place of business

(12) the Contractor, if an individual, dies or becomes incapable of performing the Contract.

12.1.2 If the Contractor is more than one person, if any of the insolvency events occur in respect of any of them, the Employer may either

(1) terminate the Contractor's obligation to complete the Works or

(2) terminate the obligation to complete the Works of the person concerned and the others shall remain liable to perform the Contractor's obligations.

12.1.3 If any insolvency events occur in respect of any person who has guaranteed the Contractor's performance of the Contract to the Employer, or a guarantee ceases to be Enforceable against the guarantor, the Employer may terminate the Contractor's obligation complete the Works unless, within 10 working days of the event, the Contractor has arranged a replacement guarantee and guarantor to the Employer's satisfaction.

Note

Grounds for termination by the Employer are:

(i) The Contractor fails to comply with his obligations under the Contract;

(ii) The Contractor suspends or abandons the Works;

(iii) The Contractor fails to proceed regularly and diligently;

(iv) The Contractor fails to provide the required insurances or performance bond;

(v) The starting has not occurred or the Contractor has not commenced the Works on site within six weeks of the Contract Date;

(vi) Any of the Contractor's warranties in sub-clause 2.5.2 (Safety, Health and Welfare) or sub-clause 2.6 (Ethics in Public Office) are untrue;

(vii) The Contractor committed or caused the Employer to commit a serious breach of Legal Requirements in relation to the Works;

(viii) The Contractor omitted a breach of the Safety Health and Welfare at Work Act 2005;

(ix) The Contractor has not complied with sub-clause 5.3.2 or 5.3.3 (Pay and Conditions of Employment);

(x) The Contractor has subcontracted all or part of the Works in breach of the Contract;

(xi) Insolvency (eight issues);

(xii) The Contractor, if an individual, dies or becomes incapable of performing the Contract.

12.2 Consequences of Default Termination

If the Contractor's obligation to complete the Works is terminated under sub-clause 12.1, the following shall apply:

12.2.1 The Contractor shall leave the Site in an orderly manner.

12.2.2 Payment of all sums of money that may then be due from the Employer to the Contractor shall be postponed, and the Employer shall not be required to make any further payment to the Contractor except as provided in this sub-clause.

12.2.3 The Employer's Representative shall, as soon as practicable, determine the amount due to the Contractor under the Contract for the Works completed in accordance with the Contract and unpaid (the **termination value**).

12.2.4 The Contractor shall not remove any Works Items or Contractor's Things from the Site unless directed to do so by the Employer, and if directed, shall promptly remove from the Site any Works Items and Contractor's Things, as directed.

12.2.5 The Employer may engage other contractors, use any Works Items and Contractor's Things on the Site and do anything necessary for the completion of the Works.

12.2.6 The Contractor shall, if so directed by the Employer's Representative, assign to the Employer [without further payment] the benefit of any subcontract, contract for the supply of any Works Item, or other contract concerning the Contract.

12.2.7 The Employer may pay to any Subcontractor or supplier to the Contractor any amount due to it that the Employer's Representative certifies as included in any previous interim payment to the Contractor. The Contractor shall re-pay to the Employer such an amount on request.

12.2.8 The Contractor shall give the Employer all Works Requirements and Contractor's Documents it [or Contractor's Personnel] has.

12.2.9 When the Works have been completed and the termination amount as described below has been determined, the Employer's Representative shall give a certificate to the Contractor and the Employer setting out the total of the following (the **termination amount**):

(1) the Employer's additional cost of completing the Works compared with the cost that would have been incurred if the Works had been completed by the Contractor in accordance with the Contract

(2) loss and damage incurred by the Employer as a result of the termination and its cause

(3) amounts due to the Employer by the Contractor under or in connection with the Contract or in connection with the Works.

12.2.10 If the Employer does not begin to put in place arrangements to complete the Works within 6 months after the termination, the Employer's Representative shall issue this certificate as soon as practicable after the end of this 6 month period, based, if necessary, on estimates.

12.2.11 If the termination amount is less than the termination value, the Contractor shall issue an invoice to the Employer for the difference and the Employer shall pay the amount due on the invoice within 15 working days after receiving the invoice. If the termination amount is more than the termination value, the Contractor shall pay the Employer the difference within 10 working days of receiving the Employer's demand for payment.

Note

The consequences of default termination are:

(i) The Contractor is obliged to leave the site in an orderly manner;

(ii) Payment of any monies due to the Contractor are postponed and the Employer shall not be required to make any further payment to the Contractor except as provided in clause 12.2;

(iii) The Employer's Representative, as soon as is practicable, make an assessment of the amount due to the Contractor in respect of Works completed in accordance with the Contract and unpaid. This is the Termination Value;

(iv) The Contractor cannot remove any Works Items or things from the site unless instructed to do so by the Employer;

(v) The Employer may engage other Contractors, use any Works Items and Contractor's Things on the site and do any thing necessary for the completion of the Works;

(vi) If instructed by the Employer's Representative, the Contractor shall assign to the Employer, without further payment, the benefit of any subcontract, contract for supply, or other contract in relation to the performance of the Works;

(vii) The Employer may pay to any subcontractor or supplier to the Contractor any amount due to it that the Employer's Representative certifies as included in any previous interim payment. The Contractor shall repay to the Employer such an amount on request;

(viii) The Contractor provides to the Employer all Work Requirements and Contractor's Documents;

(ix) When the Works have been completed and the *Termination Amount* has been assessed, the Employer's Representative shall certify the Termination Amount setting out:

a the Employer's additional cost of completing the Works compared with the cost that would have been incurred if the Works had been completed by the Contractor;

b Loss and damage incurred by the Employer as a result of the termination and its cause;

c Amounts due to the Employer by the Contractor.

(x) If the Employer does not begin to put in place arrangements for the completion of the Works within six months of the termination, the Employer's Representative shall issue the certificate as soon as possible, after the end of the six-month period based, where necessary, on estimates. If the *Termination Amount* is less than the *Termination Value* the Contractor shall raise an invoice for the difference and the Employer shall pay that amount within 15 days of receipt of the invoice. If the *Termination Amount* is more than the *Termination Value* the Contractor shall pay to the Employer the difference within 10 working days of receiving the Employer's demand for payment.

12.3 Suspension by the Contractor

If the Employer fails to pay any amount due under clause 11, the Contractor may, on giving notice to the Employer, in accordance with the Construction Contracts Act 2013, suspend execution of the Works until the amount has been paid. On receiving the payment or notice has been served by either Party referring the dispute to Adjudication, the Contractor shall resume execution of the Works.

Note
The Contractor's right to payment under certain circumstances are protected by the Construction Contracts Act 2013.

12.4 Termination by the Contractor

The Contractor shall be entitled to terminate the Contractor's obligation to complete the Works by notice to the Employer if any of the following occur:

(1) the Contractor has suspended the execution of the Works for 15 working days in accordance with sub-clause 12.3, and the Employer has still not paid

(2) work has been suspended by direction of the Employer's Representative under sub-clause 9.2 and a right to terminate has arisen under that sub-clause

(3) the execution of the Works or a substantial part of the Works has been suspended for a period of at least 3 months as a consequence of loss or damage that is at the Employer's risk under sub-clause 3.1

(4) an event or circumstance outside the control of the Parties makes it physically impossible or contrary to Law for the Contractor to fulfil its obligations under the Contract for a period of at least 6 months.

Note
The Contractor may terminate by notice to the Employer if:

(i) The Contractor has suspended the Works for 15 working days in accordance with sub-clause 12.3 (Suspension by the Contractor) and the payment has not been made;

(ii) Work has been suspended under an instruction by the Employer's Representative under sub-clause 9.2 (Suspension) and a right to terminate has arisen under that sub-clause;

(iii) Work or a substantial part of it has been suspended for a period at least three months as a consequence of loss or damage that is at the Employer's risk;

(iv) An event occurs that is outside the control of the parties and that makes it physically impossible or contrary to law for the Contractor to fulfil his obligations for a period of at least 6 months.

12.5 Termination at Employer's Election

12.5.1 The Employer shall be entitled to terminate the Contractor's obligation to complete the Works at its election on 20 working days notice to the Contractor.

12.5.2 The Employer may not terminate the Contractor's obligation to complete the Works under this sub-clause 12.5 for the purpose of retaining another contractor to execute the Works.

12.5.3 The Employer shall return any performance bond required under this Contract to the Contractor on termination under this sub-clause 12.5.

Note
The Employer is entitled to terminate the Contract upon 20 days' notice to the Contractor. The Employer cannot engage another Contractor to complete the Works. The Employer must return the performance bond to the Contractor.

12.6 Consequences of Termination by Contractor or at Employer's Election

If the Contractor's obligation to complete the Works is terminated under sub-clause 12.4 or sub-clause 12.5 the following shall apply:

12.6.1 The Contractor shall leave the Site in an orderly manner and remove any Contractor's Things.

12.6.2 The Contractor shall give the Employer all Works Requirements and all Contractors' Documents.

12.6.3 The Contractor shall, as soon as practicable, give the Employer's Representative a statement of the total of the following (the **termination sum**):

(1) the unpaid value of the parts of the Works completed to the date of termination in accordance with the Pricing Document, disregarding any provision limiting the Employer's obligation to pay for partially completed work

(2) the Contractor's reasonable costs of removal from the Site as a consequence of the termination

(3) all other amounts due to the Contractor under the Contract but not damages.

12.6.4 Within 10 working days of receiving this statement, the Employer's Representative shall issue a certificate to the Contractor and the Employer of the amount due from the Contractor to the Employer or the Employer to the Contractor, including the termination sum in the calculation of the amount due from the Employer to the Contractor. If the certificate shows an amount owing to the Contractor, the Contractor shall issue an invoice to the Employer for that amount, and the Employer shall pay the amount due on the invoice within 15 working days after receiving the invoice. If the certificate shows an amount due to the Employer, the Contractor shall pay the amount due within 10 working days of receiving the Employer's demand for payment.

Note
The following shall apply as a consequence of Termination by Contractor or at Employer's Election:

(i) The Contractor shall as soon as practicable provide the Employer's Representative with a statement of the following (the Termination Sum):

a the unpaid value of the Works completed to the date of the termination;

b the Contractor's reasonable costs of removal from site as a result of the termination;

c all other amounts to which the Contractor is entitled under the Contract.

(ii) Within 10 working of receipt of the statement the Employer's Representative shall issue a certificate indicating the amount due from the Contractor to the Employer or the amount from the Employer to the Contractor. The Contractor shall issue an invoice to the Employer and the Employer shall pay the Contractor within 15 working days of receipt of the invoice. In the event of an amount due to the Employer the Contractor shall pay that amount within 10 working days of receiving the Employer's demand;

(iii) After termination of the Contract the Contractor's obligations survive;

(iv) The Employer's liability to the Contractor is limited to the amount payable under clause 12 and any other amount that fell due under the Contract before the termination.

12.7 Survival

Termination of the Contractor's obligation to complete the Works shall not affect the Contractor's obligations under the Contract, other than the obligation to complete the Works. [In particular the following provisions of the Contract continue to have effect after termination: sub-clauses 1.1, 1.2, 1.3, 1.4, 1.7, 1.8, 1.9, 2.1, 2.6, 3.4, 3.5, 4.16, 4.17, clause 6, this clause 12 and clause 13.]

12.8 Payment

On termination of the Contractor's obligation to complete the Works, the Employer's liability to the Contractor under or in connection with the Contract shall be limited to payment of the amount provided for in this clause 12, and any other amount that fell due under the Contract before the termination.

12.9 Reference to Conciliation

12.9.1 The Employer may [but is not required to] refer to conciliation under sub-clause 13.2 the issue of whether the Employer has become entitled to terminate the Contractor's obligation to complete the Works under sub-clause 12.1.

12.9.2 Sub-clause 13.2 shall apply to the conciliation, except that the conciliator's time to give the recommendation shall be 21 days after appointment. Clause 13.5 shall also apply.

12.9.3 If the conciliator recommends that the Employer is entitled to terminate the Contractor's obligation to complete the Works under sub-clause 12.1, and the Employer does so within 63 days after receiving the conciliator's recommendation, and it is subsequently found that the Employer was not entitled to do so, then the following shall apply:

(1) the termination shall stand [even if the circumstances have changed] and have effect as if the Employer's termination notice under sub-clause 12.1 was a valid termination notice under sub-clause 12.5.1

(2) sub-clauses 12.6.1 to 12.6.4 inclusive shall apply retrospectively from the date of the termination notice under sub-clause 12.1

(3) sub-clause 12.5.2 shall not apply

(4) the Contractor shall have no other rights or remedies under the Contract or otherwise at law for the termination.

Note

The Employer may refer to conciliation the issue of whether the Employer has become entitled to terminate the Contractor's obligations. The conciliator's time to give his recommendation is 21 days after his appointment. If it was subsequently found that the Employer was not entitled to terminate the Contractor's obligations then:

(i) The termination shall stand;

(ii) Sub-clauses 12.6.1 to 12.6.4 (Consequences of Termination by Contractor or at Employer's Election) shall apply retrospectively from the date of the termination notice;

(iii) Sub-clause 12.5.2 shall not apply;

(iv) The Contractor shall have no other rights or remedies under the Contract or otherwise at law.

If the conciliator agrees that a termination breach has occurred, the Employer decides whether or not he will act on that determination. If the Employer decides to terminate and an Arbitrator subsequently finds that the decision to terminate was incorrect, the rights of the Contractor are restricted to the rights the Contractor would have had if the Contract had been terminated at the election of the Employer, that is, the value of works to date and reasonable demobilisation costs.

13 DISPUTES

13.1 Dispute Management Procedure

13.1.1 If a dispute arises under sub-clause 10.5.4 or 10.5.5 of the Contract, either Party may, by notice to the other, refer the dispute for resolution under this sub-clause 13.1. The notice shall state that the dispute is given under sub-clause 13.1 of the Contract.

13.1.2 The dispute management procedure for resolution of disputes arising under sub-clause 10.5.4 or 10.5.5 of the Contract consists of meetings of the Project Board as detailed in this Clause.

The Project Board:

(1) shall meet at least every 60 days to review disputes referred under clause 13.1 and may, by agreement of the Project Board, call an interim Project Board Meeting sooner than the next scheduled date for a Project Board Meeting, to review disputes referred. Where no disputes are referred the Project Board may, by agreement of the Project Board, defer scheduled Project Board meetings until a dispute arises under clause 13.1. There shall be a minimum of 1 member from each Party and a maximum of 3 members from each Party, as named in Schedule Part 3A, at all Project Board meetings;

(2) shall ensure that all unresolved disputes at the end of a scheduled Project Board Meeting or interim Project Board Meeting are so notified to the Parties on the next Working Day after the Project Board meeting ("date of notification"). Either Party may refer such unresolved disputes to conciliation [in accordance with sub-clause 13.2] within 14 days of the date of notification to the Parties by the Project Board, otherwise the Employer's Representative's determination issued under sub-clause 10.5 shall be binding;

(3) shall communicate orally or in writing on a "without prejudice" basis, including all communications between the Project Board members and to the Standing Conciliator, [where appointed], and such communications may not be relied upon by either Party in subsequent dispute resolution proceedings under this Contract, other than the signed agreement as set out in sub-clause 13.1.2.(4);

(4) shall ensure all agreements to resolve a dispute between the Parties are in writing and signed by the Parties. This agreement is binding on the Parties;

(5) may, where the relevant appointment has been made, agree to have the Standing Conciliator or conciliator draft the binding agreement to be signed by the Parties. If the agreement is not signed by both Parties within 14 days of the date of issue of the agreement by the Standing Conciliator or conciliator, either Party may refer the dispute to conciliation as per 13.1.2(2) above within a further 14 days. If the dispute is not referred to Conciliation within this further 14 day period the Employer's Representative determination issued under sub-clause 10.5 shall be binding;

(6) may agree to have the Standing Conciliator, where one has been appointed, attend or chair the Project Board meetings;

(7) may agree to seek advice or opinion from the Standing Conciliator at the Project Board meeting, where one is appointed, either orally or in writing , in an effort to resolve disputes referred.

Note

The Dispute Management Procedure, (DMP), is a new dispute resolution process under the Contract that was brought about as an amendment following the review of the Public Works Contracts. The review proposed a number of interim amendments amongst which was the inclusion of informal dispute resolution methods to reduce the volume of disputes that are currently being referred to the formal procedures prescribed in the Contract.

For all projects carried out under Public Works Contract Form PW-CF1 to PW- CF4 inclusive the Parties to the Contract may engage in a, without prejudice, dispute resolution process on certain disputes prior to reference to conciliation. Sub-clause 13.1 of the Conditions of Contract details the Dispute Management Procedure for resolution of disputed Employer's Representative Determinations issued under Sub-clause 10.5.4 and 10.5.5 of the Conditions of Contract. The procedure shall consist of meetings of the Project Board, as defined under Sub-clause 13.1.2 of the Contract, for the purpose of reviewing disputes referred thereto with the intent of reaching a resolution.

Details of the Project Board are set out in the Office of Government Procurement Guidance Notes 3.1.1 as can be found at:
http://constructionprocurement.gov.ie/wp-content/uploads/GN-3.1.1v1.0-22-01-2016.pdf

13.2 Conciliation

Where Schedule Part 1N so states that a Standing Conciliator shall be appointed, the Standing Conciliator shall take the place of the conciliator under sub-clause 13.2 for all disputes referred to conciliation under sub-clause 13.2]

13.2.1 If a dispute arises under the Contract, [or where a dispute referred to the dispute management procedure has not been resolved], either Party may, by notice to the other, refer the dispute for conciliation under this sub-clause 13.2. The notice shall state that it is given under sub-clause 13.2 of the Contract. [No dispute referred to the dispute management procedure may be referred to conciliation without first completing the dispute management procedure.]

13.2.2 Except in the case where a Standing Conciliator has been appointed, [and in such cases the Standing Conciliator shall be the conciliator], within 10 working days of the referral of a dispute to conciliation, the Parties shall jointly appoint a conciliator who is competent to adjudicate upon the dispute and independent of the Parties. If the Parties fail to appoint a conciliator within 10 working days of the referral, or if a person appointed refuses to act or becomes unable to act, the conciliator shall be appointed by the appointing body or person named in the Schedule, part 1N, on the application of either Party. If there is a fee for making the appointment, the Parties shall share it equally. If one Party pays the entire fee, it shall be entitled to reimbursement of the other Party's share from the other Party on demand.

13.2.3 Each Party shall, within the period set by the conciliator, send to the conciliator and the other Party brief details of the dispute stating its contentions as to the facts and the Parties' rights and obligations concerning the dispute. The conciliator may, for this purpose, suggest further actions or investigations that may be of assistance.

13.2.4 The Parties shall promptly make available to the conciliator all information, documents, access to the Site and appropriate facilities that the conciliator requires to resolve the dispute.

13.2.5 The conciliator shall consult with the Parties in an attempt to resolve the dispute by agreement. The conciliator may do any of the following, or any combination of them:

(1) meet the Parties separately from each other or together and consider documents from one Party not sent or shown to the other

(2) conduct investigations in the absence of the Parties

(3) make use of specialist knowledge

(4) obtain technical or legal advice

(5) establish the procedures to be followed in the conciliation

Where the dispute has been referred to the dispute management procedure and Sub-clause 13.1.2(5) and 13.1.2(6) of the Contract applies, the conciliator, with the agreement of the Parties, may forgo the requirements of 13.2.5(1) to 13.2.5(5) inclusive and give the Parties a written recommendation in accordance with 13.2.8.

13.2.6 The conciliator shall not be an arbitrator and the Arbitration Act 2010 and the law relating to arbitration shall not apply to the conciliation.

13.2.7 The conciliator's terms of appointment shall be those in the Works Requirements or, if there are none, those agreed by the Employer and the Contractor with the conciliator.

13.2.8 If the dispute is not resolved by agreement within 42 days after the conciliator was appointed, [or after referral of the dispute to conciliation where a Standing Conciliator has been appointed], or a longer period proposed by the conciliator and agreed by the Parties, the conciliator shall give both Parties a written recommendation. The conciliator shall base the recommendation on the Parties' rights and obligations under the Contract.

13.2.9 If either Party is dissatisfied with the conciliator's recommendation, it may, within 42 days after receiving the conciliator's recommendation, so notify the other Party. The notice shall state that it is given under sub-clause 13.2 of the Contract, and shall state the matters in dispute and the reasons for dissatisfaction. If the conciliator has failed to give a recommendation within 42 days after appointment, either Party may give a notice of dissatisfaction. If notice of dissatisfaction has been given in accordance with this clause, either Party may refer the dispute to arbitration under sub-clause 13.4.

13.2.10 If neither Party gives notice of dissatisfaction within 42 days after receiving the conciliator's recommendation, the recommendation shall be conclusive and binding on the Parties, and the Parties agree to comply with it. If, in such circumstances, a Party fails to comply with the conciliator's recommendation, the other Party may [without limiting its other rights] refer the failure itself to Adjudication, [where the dispute is a dispute relating to payment], or to arbitration under sub-clause 13.4, and need not invoke this sub-clause 13.2 for this reference.

13.2.11 If the conciliator has recommended the payment of money and a notice of dissatisfaction is given, the following shall apply:

(1) The Party concerned shall make the payment recommended by the conciliator, provided that the other Party first
   (a) gave a notice, complying with the arbitration rules referred to in sub-clause 13.4, referring the same dispute to arbitration and
   (b) gave the paying Party a bond executed by a surety approved by the paying Party, acting reasonably, in the form included in the Works Requirements, or if there is none, a form approved by the paying Party, acting reasonably, for the amount of the payment.

(2) If, when the dispute is finally resolved, it is found that the Party receiving payment on the conciliator's recommendation was not entitled to some or all of the amount paid, then that Party shall repay the amount it was paid and found not to be entitled to, together with interest.

(3) When the dispute is finally resolved, interest will be deducted from final payment under the award or judgment.

(4) Interest under this sub-clause is calculated at the reference rate referred to in the European Communities (Late Payment in Commercial Transactions) Regulations 2012 plus 2% per year and runs from the date of the original payment to the date of the repayment or final payment.

(5) [This provision for interest is confidential under sub-clause 13.2.12, and in particular shall not be taken into account or referred to in arbitration until all other matters are resolved.]

13.2.12 The conciliation shall be confidential, and the Parties shall respect its confidentiality, except when any of the exceptions in sub-clause 4.16 apply, or to the extent necessary to enforce a recommendation that has become conclusive and binding. All documents provided by a Party in connection with a conciliation shall be returned when the conciliation is concluded.

Note
Sub-clause 13.2 of the PW-CF1 to PW-CF5 details the process and procedures of conciliation for use under these forms of Contract. The process may be commenced by either Party following referral of a dispute in accordance with sub-clause 13.2.1 of the Contract. The notice of referral shall state that it is given under sub-clause 13.2 and shall be notified to the named individual in Schedule Part 1A or Schedule Part 2A of the Contract.

The appointment of the Conciliator should be effected through the use of Model Form 1.16 *Appointment of Conciliator.*

Details of the Conciliation procedures, including the role of the Standing Conciliator are set out in the Office of Government Procurement Guidance Notes 3.1.1 as can be found at: http://constructionprocurement.gov.ie/wp-content/uploads/GN-3.1.1v1.0-22-01-2016.pdf.

13.3 Adjudication

13.3.1 The parties have recourse to Adjudication in accordance with the Construction Contracts Act 2013

13.3.2 Where an adjudicator reaches a decision on a dispute referred under the Construction Contracts Act 2013, that same dispute shall not be referred to the dispute management procedure or conciliation under the Contract.

13.3.3 If a dispute between the Parties is referred to Adjudication, any dispute management procedure or conciliation relating to that dispute immediately adjourns. In the event that no decision is reached by the adjudicator, the parties may continue to resolve the dispute under the dispute management procedure or conciliation from the date the dispute was referred to Adjudication. In the event that a decision is reached by the adjudicator, the dispute management procedure or conciliation for that dispute shall be terminated.

Note
All contracts entered into on or after the 25 July 2016 are subject to statutory adjudication under the Construction Contracts Act 2013. Adjudications can be sought by either party at any time during the course Works. Decisions of the adjudicator are final and binding in the interim.

A copy of the Construction Contracts Act 2013 can be found at: http://www.irishstatutebook.ie/eli/2013/act/34/enacted/en/html

13.4 Arbitration

Any dispute that, under sub-clause 13.2, may be referred to conciliation shall, subject to sub-clause 13.2 be finally settled by arbitration in accordance with the arbitration rules identified in the Schedule, part 1N. For purposes of those rules, the person or body to appoint the arbitrator, if not agreed by the Parties, is named in the Schedule, part 1N.

Note
Arbitration is the final stage for resolution of construction disputes and is incorporated into the Public Works Contracts.

In Ireland, arbitration is governed by the Arbitration Act 2010. Arbitrations arising out of the Public Works Contract For Building Works Designed By The Employer are conducted under the Capital Works Management Framework Arbitration Rules for Use with Public Works and Construction Services Contracts – AR 1.

A copy of the Capital Works Management Framework Arbitration Rules for Use with Public Works and Construction Services Contracts – AR 1 as can be found at: http://www.constructionprocurement.gov.ie/wp-content/uploads/Arbitration-Rules.pdf.

13.5 Jurisdiction

Subject to the above provisions of this clause, the Parties submit to the jurisdiction of the Irish courts to settle any dispute that may arise out of or in connection with the Contract or the Works.

The Public Works forms of Contract have varying requirements with regards use of the Irish Courts:

- PW-CF1 to PW-CF5 requires the Parties to submit to the jurisdiction of the Irish Courts for disputes arising out of, or in connection with the Contract, whereas disputes under the Contract shall be ultimately resolved at Arbitration
- PW-CF6, PW-CF8 and PW-CF11 requires the Parties to submit to the jurisdiction of the Irish Courts.

PW-CF7 and PW-CF10 requires the Parties to submit to the jurisdiction of the Irish Courts but requires that disputes under the Contract shall be ultimately resolved at Arbitration

13.6 Agent for Service

If an agent for service of legal proceedings on the Contractor is named in part 2A of the Schedule, the Contractor confirms to the Employer that it has irrevocably appointed the named person as its agent for the service of all documents relating to legal proceedings, and that failure of the agent to notify the Contractor of receipt of a document will not invalidate any proceedings or the service of the document.

13.7 Continuing Obligations

[Despite the existence of a dispute, the Parties shall continue to perform their obligations under the Contract.]

End of Conditions.

OPTIONAL CLAUSES PV1 AND PV2

OPTIONAL CLAUSES PV1 AND PV2

PV1 PRICE VARIATION

PV1.1 Contract Sum Adjustment

The Contract Sum is adjusted for fluctuations in costs of resources only in respect of increases or decreases that occur in workers' wages or expenses, or material prices, or are made by Law, as follows:

PV1.1.1 Timing:

(a) The **Base Date** means the first day of the 31st month after the Contract Date.

Note
Contractors should be aware that the Base Date is the first day of the 31st month after the Contract Date, rather than the Designated Date as defined in Sub-Clause 1.1 of the Conditions. There can be a substantial period of time between the date that tenders are returned and the actual Contract Date.

(b) No increase or decrease that comes into being after the Date for Substantial Completion shall be taken into account for the purpose of this clause PV1.

PV1.1.2 Workers' wages and expenses

The Contract Sum shall be adjusted by the amount of an increase or decrease in workers' wages or expenses that satisfies all these requirements:

(i) it is made to the standard normal and overtime hourly wage rates or expenses payable to workers according to the Labour Court's Registered Employment Agreement dated 15 March 1967 as varied from time to time under Section 28 of the Industrial Relations Act 1946 and

(ii) it becomes payable after the Base Date in accordance with that agreement and

(iii) it is in respect of General Round Increases conforming to the guidelines of the Social Partnership Agreements between the government, employer organisations and trade unions relating to such increases, or, in the absence of a Social Partnership Agreement and guidelines, increases in accordance with the guidelines on General Round Increases issued by the Department of Finance and

(iv) the workers in respect of whom an increase is being claimed have received in Ireland for the relevant work at least the increased standard wage rates and expenses.

Workers means

(a) craftspersons and

(b) semi-skilled and unskilled labour and

(c) drivers and operators of plant and machinery and

(d) time-keepers and clerical staff stationed on site and

(e) any foreperson, charge hand or other person who supervises or administers while performing duties within (a) – (c), but in respect only of the standard wage rates according to sub-clause PV1.1.2(i) and expenses applicable to those duties and 50% of their total hours worked.

[Site agents, managers, other full time supervisors and administrators, and surveyors, for example, are excluded.]

General Round Increases means increases in workers' wages to the extent that they apply generally in the construction industry and are compliant with Government guidelines and Social Partnership Agreements.

Expenses means expenses payable for country money and PRSI payable by the Contractor as employer.

[All other increases are excluded, even where calculated as a percentage of a standard rate. So, for example, the Contractor is not entitled to any payment for local or site bargaining provisions; any parity or restructuring increases; any bonus under a site agreement, productivity, incentive, or other bonus; insurance premiums, other on-costs or consequential costs].

PV1.1.3 Materials

The Contract Sum shall be adjusted by the amount of an increase or decrease in the Price of material that results from either or both of these calculations where applicable:

- So far as the Price of any material at the Purchase Date has increased by more than 50 percent of the Price at the first business day of the month in which the purchase occurred or the Price at the Designated Date (whichever is highest) then that excess percentage over 50 percent is applied to its Price at the Designated Date.
- So far as the Price of any material at the Base Date has increased or decreased at the Purchase Date by more than 10 percent, then that excess percentage over 10 percent is applied to the Price at the Base Date.

Material means only

(a) material invoiced to the project

(b) for incorporation in the permanent Works [as fixtures or unfixed goods],

(c) or for temporary works used on the Site

(d) and not used on any previous project or usable on any subsequent one [for example, replaceable components in formwork]. [Tools or equipment are not 'material'. There is no deduction of normal wastage from the allowable quantity of material, or of extra or surplus material taken over by the Employer].

Purchase Date means the date when the particular material was invoiced to the project.

Price means the average price at which the relevant volume of the relevant material is available in the market at the relevant time from a representative number of reputable manufacturers or suppliers.

[There is no adjustment for any alteration in the price of material except as specified in this sub-clause].

PV1.1.4 Law

The Contract Sum shall be adjusted by the amount of any increase or decrease in the Contractor's cost of performing its obligations under the Contract as a result of a change in Law made after the Designated Date that

(i) changes [whether by alteration, addition or removal] VAT, customs or excise duties, requirements for a licence to import or export any commodity or Pay- Related Social Insurance and

(ii) is not identified in the Works Requirements and

(iii) has not resulted in an adjustment in the Contract Sum under another part of this clause PV1 or the Contract.

PV1.2 Communications

The Contractor shall maintain arrangements to become aware of any significant possibility of an increase or decrease in the Contract Sum that may arise in accordance with this clause PV1 and shall immediately notify the Employer's Representative of any such possibility and keep him informed of any opportunities to minimise an increase.

PV1.3 Compensation Events

The Pricing Document and the valuation rules in sub-clause 10.6 shall not cease to determine, apply to or be the basis of the valuation of a Compensation Event by reason of price fluctuations in material costs, but the following principles shall apply -

(i) No departure from rates in the Pricing Document shall be made in respect of fluctuations affecting the cost of material omitted by a Change Order.

(ii) Valuation of a Change Order shall include any increase in the cost to the Contractor of material substituted or added by the Change Order that is due to price fluctuation after the Designated Date so far as it is likely to exceed the price fluctuation increase that under this clause PV1 would have been the Contractor's risk for the original material.

No adjustment under this clause PV1 shall apply to an adjustment or the part of an adjustment of the Contract Sum valued under sub-clauses 10.6.4 or 10.7.

PV1.4 Efficiency

[In addition to sub-clause PV1.1.1(b),] increases of the Contract Sum will only apply so far as the increased costs incurred by the Contractor occur despite its efficient progress and procurement and reasonable efforts to minimise increases.

PV1.5 Certificates & Payment

The Contractor shall fully detail and vouch any fluctuations in costs relevant to this clause PV1 as soon as practicable, and they shall then be allowed for in interim and final certificates and payments under and subject to clause 11.

PV2 PRICE VARIATION

PV2.1 Definitions

For the purpose of this clause definitions are set out in Appendix 1 [as well as elsewhere in the Conditions].

PV2.2 Contract Sum Adjustment

The Contract Sum, excluding the amount of Non-Adjustable Overheads, shall be subject to adjustment for price fluctuations or changes in Law only in the circumstances set out in this clause PV2. No increase or decrease shall be made in respect of any amount that relates to works before the Base Date except as provided in sub-clauses PV2.4 and PV2.8.4.

PV2.3 Proportions

For the purpose of calculating adjustments to the Contract Sum, the proportions of Labour, Materials, Fuel, Non-Reusable Temporary Works and Non-Adjustable Overheads in the Contract Sum are set out in Appendix 7 [irrespective of the actual proportions of the work].

PV2.4 Change in Law

The Contract Sum shall be adjusted by the amount of any increase or decrease in the Contractor's cost of performing its obligations under the Contract as a result of a change in Law made after the Designated Date, or if a Recovery date has been agreed or determined, made after the Recovery Date, but before the Date for Substantial Completion of the Works or a Section, that

(i) changes [whether by alteration, addition or removal] VAT, customs or excise duties, requirements for a licence to import or export any commodity or Pay-Related Social Insurance and

(ii) is not identified in the Works Requirements and

(iii) has not resulted in an adjustment in the Contract Sum under another part of this clause PV2 or the Contract.

PV2.5 Failure to Complete on Time

If the Contractor fails to complete the Works or a Section by its Date for Substantial Completion, adjustment of the Contract Sum in respect of the Works or Section after its Date for Substantial Completion shall be effected by the Index Figures, General Round Increases or Consumer Price Index applicable to the Adjustment Period in which the Date for Substantial Completion occurs.

PV2.6 Excluded Amounts

The following are not subject to price adjustment (**Excluded Amounts**):

(a) Delay cost under sub-clause 10.7

(b) Adjustments or parts of adjustments of the Contract Sum valued under sub-clause 10.6.4

(c) Amounts for unfixed materials or goods for which the Contractor is entitled to payment under sub-clause 11.2

(d) Amounts based on actual costs or current prices

(e) Credits allowed for old materials arising from the Works

(f) Amounts for work executed under an agreement containing specific price arrangements

(g) Costs incurred for making good defects under clause 8

(h) [In addition to sub-clause PV2.5] amounts by which any cost incurred by the Contractor has been increased by a default of the Contractor.

PV2.7 Revisions of Index Figures

If an Index Figure used for a Material Category or a Fuel Category or the Consumer Price Index in relation to Non-Reusable Temporary Works is subsequently revised by the Central Statistics Office prior to the issue of the Final Certificate, any adjustments in accordance with this Clause shall be recalculated on the basis of the revised Index Figures.

PV2.8 Materials and Fuel

PV2.8.1 Weightings

For the purpose of calculating any adjustments to the amount payable in respect of Materials and Fuel in an Interim or Final Certificate, the weightings of Material and Fuel Categories in the Contract Sum are set out in Part I or Part II of Appendix 8, as applicable [irrespective of the actual constituents, weightings or proportions of the work].

PV2.8.2 Materials

Subject to sub-clause PV2.8.4, the amount payable in respect of Materials in an Interim Certificate or in the Final Certificate (other than amounts for price adjustments under this clause PV2 or any Excluded Amounts) in respect of an Adjustment Period shall be increased or decreased in accordance with the provisions of this clause PV2, and the total adjustment to the amount payable in such Interim Certificate or in the Final Certificate in respect of Materials shall be equal to the sum of the adjustments for each Material Category, which adjustments shall be calculated using the relevant formula set out in Appendix 2.

PV2.8.3 Fuel

Subject to sub-clause PV2.8.4, the amount payable in respect of the Fuel Percentage of an Interim Certificate or of the Final Certificate (other than amounts for price adjustments under this clause PV2 or any Excluded Amounts) in respect of an Adjustment Period shall be increased or decreased in accordance with the provisions of this clause PV2, and the total adjustment to the amount payable in such Interim Certificate or in the Final Certificate in respect of the Fuel Percentage shall be equal to the sum of the adjustments for each Fuel Category, which adjustments shall be calculated using the relevant formula set out in Appendix 3.

PV2.8.4 Exceptional Increases for Materials and Fuel

The amount payable in respect of a Material and/or the Fuel Percentage in an Interim Certificate or in the Final Certificate (other than amounts for price adjustments under this clause PV2 or any Excluded Amounts) may be increased for any Exceptional Increase in respect of that Material and/or Fuel after the Designated Date, or, if a Recovery Date has been agreed or determined, after the Recovery Date calculated using the relevant formula for Materials or Fuel set out in Appendix 4, as appropriate, **provided however** that adjustment of the Contract Sum under this sub-clause in respect of works after the Base Date shall be effected by the greater of the increase calculated in accordance with this sub-clause PV2.8.4 and the relevant increase calculated in accordance with sub-clause PV2.8.2 in respect of that Material or in accordance with sub-clause PV2.8.3 in respect of that Fuel.

PV2.8.5 Non-Reusable Temporary Works

The amount payable in respect of Non-Reusable Temporary Works in an Interim Certificate or the Final Certificate (other than amounts for price adjustments under this clause PV2 or any Excluded Amounts) issued in respect of an Adjustment Period shall be adjusted in accordance with the relevant formula set out in Appendix 5.

PV2.8.6 Labour

The amount payable in respect of Labour in an Interim Certificate or the Final Certificate (other than amounts for price adjustments under this clause PV2 or any Excluded Amounts) issued in respect of an Adjustment Period shall be adjusted in accordance with the relevant formula set out in Appendix 6, **but only** to the extent that the workers in respect of whom an increase is being claimed have received in Ireland for the relevant work at least the increased standard wage rates.

Appendix 1 to Clause PV2

DEFINITIONS

	Term	*Meaning*
(a)	Adjustment Index Figure	the appropriate Index Figure for the Adjustment Month **provided however** that, the Index Figure for any Adjustment Month that occurs after the Date for Substantial Completion of the Works or a relevant Section shall be determined in accordance with sub-clause PV2.5.
(b)	Adjustment Month	the month during which the middle day of the Adjustment Period occurred (if the Adjustment Period is an even number of days the last day is not to be counted).
(c)	Adjustment Period	the period between the last preceding Interim Certificate and the current Interim Certificate or the Final Certificate, **provided however** that if any Certificate is calculated in respect of a period that includes works before and after the Base Date, then only that part of the period that falls after the Base Date will be the Adjustment Period for the purposes of that certificate.
(d)	Base Date	the first day of the 37th calendar month after the Designated Date, or if a Recovery Date has been agreed or determined, after the Recovery Date.
(e)	Base Index Figure	the appropriate Index Figure for the Base Month.
(f)	Base Month	the month during which the Base Date occurs.
(g)	Category	any Material Category or Non-Reusable Temporary Works.
(h)	Consumer Price Index	the consumer price index (all items) published by the Central Statistics Office, Ireland (including any successor or replacement thereof).

	Term	*Meaning*
(i)	Effective Value	the difference between (I) the amount which is due in any Interim or Final Certificate (before deducting retention) less any amounts for price adjustments and Excluded Amounts and (II) the amount included in the last preceding Interim Certificate calculated in accordance with (I) above **provided that** in the case of the first Interim Certificate the Effective Value shall be the amount calculated in accordance with (I) above, **provided however** that if any amount payable in any Interim or Final Certificate is calculated in respect of works before the Base Date, then only that part of the amount payable in such Interim or Final Certificate that refers to works after the Base Date (less any amounts for price adjustments and any Excluded Amounts) will be included in the Effective Value, except that works before the Base Date may be included in the Effective Value for the purposes only of sub-clause PV2.8.4.
(j)	Exceptional Increase	means that part of an increase that is in excess of 50% from one CSO monthly Index Figure to the next CSO monthly Index Figure for a particular Material or Fuel Category after the Designated Date or, if a Recovery Date has been agreed or determined after the Recovery Date to the extent that such increase is in excess of 50% above the CSO monthly Index Figure for that Material or Fuel Category at the Designated Date or, if a Recovery Date has been agreed or determined, at the Recovery Date.
(k)	Final Certificate	a certificate provided by the Employer's Representative in accordance with sub- clause 11.5.3.
(l)	Fuel and Fuel Category	any or all of the sources of energy listed in Part II of Appendix 8, as appropriate.
(m)	Fuel Percentage	the percentage of the Contract Sum that consists of Fuel set out in Appendix 7.
(n)	General Round Increase	increases in workers' wages to the extent that they apply to all workers in the construction industry and are compliant with Government guidelines and Social Partnership Agreements. [All other increases are excluded, even where calculated as a percentage of a standard rate. So, for example, the Contractor is not entitled to any payment for local or site bargaining provisions; any parity or restructuring increases; any bonus under a site agreement, productivity, incentive, or other bonus; PRSI, insurance premiums, or other on-costs or consequential costs.]
(o)	Index Figures	those index figures compiled by or on behalf of the Central Statistics Office, Ireland (or such other public body as is authorised to perform this function) applicable to each Material or Fuel Category listed in Appendix 8, or, where appropriate, Consumer Price Index figures.
(p)	Interim Certificate	a certificate or penultimate payment certificate provided by the Employer's Representative in accordance with sub-clause 11.1.3 or sub-clause 11.5.2.
(q)	Labour Percentage	the percentage of the Contract Sum that consists of Labour set out in Appendix 7.
(r)	Material(s) and Material Category	any or all of the materials listed in Part I of Appendix 8, as appropriate.

	Term	*Meaning*
(s)	Materials Percentage	the percentage of the Contract Sum that consists of Materials set out in Appendix 7.
(t)	Non-Adjustable Overheads	the percentage of the Contract Sum that consists of non-adjustable overheads set out in Appendix 7.
(u)	Non-Reusable Temporary Works	those Work Elements identified in the Pricing Document or Works Requirements as being non-reusable temporary works.
(v)	Non-Reusable Temporary Works Percentage	the percentage of the Contract Sum that consists of non-reusable temporary works set out in Appendix 7.
(w)	Recovery Date	the Designated Date adjusted by the period of delay to the Starting Date that results from the actions or omissions of the Contractor after the Contract Date, but prior to the Starting Date (the **Contractor's Period of Delay**) as is agreed by the Parties. If the Parties do not agree the Recovery Date then the Employer may deliver to the Employer's Representative full and detailed particulars of any claim to a Contractor's Period of Delay and the Recovery Date shall be the Designated Date adjusted by the Contractor's Period of Delay, if any, that the Employer's Representative certifies as fair and reasonable.
(x)	Work Element	a constituent of the work in the Pricing Document, or such other tender document as appropriate, for which the Employer's Representative has identified a corresponding Material Category or that forms part of the Non-Reusable Temporary Works, and which is not an Excluded Amount, **provided however** that no work before the Base Date shall form part of a Work Element for the purposes of adjustment in accordance with this Clause, with the exception of sub-clause PV2.8.4.

Appendix 2 to Clause PV2

MATERIALS

The formulae for price fluctuations in Material Categories pursuant to sub-clause PV2.8.2 are as follows:

A. ***Formula to be used where A1 – B1 is less than or equal to zero:***

W x Y x Z x P x (A1 – B1)/B1 = K

B. ***Formula to be used where A1 – B1 is greater than zero:***

{W x Y x Z x P x (A1 – B1)/B1} – (10% x W x Y x Z x P) = K

PROVIDED THAT if K under Formula B is less than zero for the relevant Material Category solely as a result of the deduction of the ten percent (10%), the adjustment for that Material Category shall be zero.

(Note: Formula B will deduct 10% from any increase in the indices and effectively sets Base Index + 10% as the threshold at which recovery starts.)

where:

W = The weighting attributed to a particular Material Category, as stated in Part I of Appendix 8.

Y = The Materials Percentage.

Z = Contract Sum (excluding VAT and any price adjustments under this Clause) less any Excluded Amounts.

P = The amount which is due in any Interim or Final Certificate for the relevant Material Category less the last amount, if any, for that Material Category included in an Interim Certificate with the resulting balance divided by the total amount for that Material Category in the Contract Sum **provided that** the aggregate value of P in respect of any Material Category calculated over the course of the contract shall not exceed 1. In the calculation of P all amounts relating to price adjustments under this Clause shall be excluded.

The amounts in the Interim Certificates and/or Final Certificate used to calculate this proportion P are those for Work Elements allocated to the relevant Material Category in the Pricing Document or other pricing document forming part of the Contract.

No amount for a Work Element (or part of a Work Element) in the Pricing Document, or other pricing document forming part of the Contract may be used for the calculation of adjustments for more than one Category.

A1 = The Adjustment Index Figure for the relevant Material Category.

B1= The Base Index Figure for the relevant Material Category.

K = The amount of increase or decrease recoverable in relation to price fluctuations for the particular Material in an Interim or Final Certificate.

Provided however that if at any time the Central Statistics Office ceases to publish Index Figures in respect of a particular Material Category then the following formula shall apply for calculating any increases or decreases in respect of that Material in any Interim Certificate and/or Final Certificate issued in respect of works after such time **provided always** that any such increases or decreases shall only apply in respect of works after the Base Date:

A. ***Formula to be used where $CPI^A - CPI^B$ is less than or equal to zero:***

$$W \times Y \times Z \times P \times (CPI^A - CPI^B)/CPI^B = K$$

B. ***Formula to be used where CPIA – CPIB is greater than zero:***

$$\{W \times Y \times Z \times P \times (CPI^A - CPI^B)/CPI^B\} - (10\% \times W \times Y \times Z \times P) = K$$

PROVIDED THAT if K under Formula B is less than zero for the relevant Material Category solely as a result of the deduction of the ten percent (10%), the adjustment for that Material Category shall be zero.

where:

CPIA = the Consumer Price Index for the Adjustment Month, subject to sub-clause PV2.5.

CPIB = the Consumer Price Index for the Base Month.

Worked Example

A four year contract is in its 44th month and material price increases occurring after the expiry of the 37th month (i.e. after the Base Date) are claimable in Interim Valuations. The 43rd Interim Valuation has included in it a claim for an increase in the price of ready mixed mortar and concrete which occurred after the Base Date. The relevant particulars are as follows:

Z	The Contract Sum (excluding VAT and any price adjustments under this Clause) less any Excluded Amounts	€6,000,000
Y	The percentage of the contract sum (excluding VAT) attributable to Materials, as stated in Appendix 7	35%
W	The weighting for ready mixed mortar and concrete in the tender documents, as stated in Appendix 8	0.2
B1	The Base Index Figure for ready mixed mortar and concrete	105.3
A1	The Adjustment Index Figure for ready mixed mortar and concrete	126.36

P	The proportion of the particular Material Category in the Contract Sum (prior to any adjustments) as accepted by the Employer's Representative being paid for in the Interim Valuation (as certified). (This percentage is arrived at by calculating the difference between the amount due in the Interim or Final Certificate for the relevant Material Category less the last amount, if any, for that Material Category in an Interim Certificate with the resulting balance divided by the total amount of that Material Category in the Contract Sum.)	25%

As A1 – B1 is greater than zero, K, the recoverable increase, is calculated using formula B, as follows:

{W x Y x Z x P x (A1 – B1)/B1} – (10% x W x Y x Z x P) = K

{.2 x .35 x 6,000,000 x .25 x (126.36 – 105.3)/105.3} – (10% x .2 x .35 x 6,000,000 x .25) = €10,500

The amount of the recoverable increase for ready mixed mortar and concrete is **€10,500**.

(This €10,500 will be added to the recoverable increase for other materials in order to determine the overall increase for materials in this certificate.)

Appendix 3 to Clause PV2

FUEL

The formulae for price fluctuations in Fuel Categories pursuant to sub-clause PV2.8.3 are as follows:

A. Formula to be used where A1 – B1 is less than or equal to zero:

W x Y x EV x (A1 – B1)/B1 = L

B. Formula to be used where A1 – B1 is greater than zero:

W x Y x EV x (A1 – B1)/B1} – (10% x W x Y x EV) = L

PROVIDED THAT if L under Formula B is less than zero for the relevant Fuel Category solely as a result of the deduction of the ten percent (10%), the adjustment for that Fuel Category shall be zero.

where:

W = The weighting attributed to a particular Fuel Category, as stated in Part II of Appendix 8.

Y = The Fuel Percentage.

EV = Effective Value (excluding VAT).

A1 = The Adjustment Index Figure for the relevant Fuel Category.

B1 = The Base Index Figure for the relevant Fuel Category.

L = The amount of increase or decrease recoverable in relation to price fluctuations in the particular Fuel Category in an Interim or Final Certificate.

Provided however that if at any time the Central Statistics Office ceases to publish Index Figures in respect of a particular Fuel Category then the following formula shall apply for calculating any increases or decreases in respect of that Fuel in any Interim Certificate and/or Final Certificate issued in respect of works after such time **provided always** that any such increases or decreases shall only apply in respect of works after the Base Date:

A. Formula to be used where CPIA – CPIB is less than or equal to zero:

W x Y x EV x (CPI^A – CPI^B)/CPI^B = L

B. Formula to be used where A1 – CPIB is greater than zero:

{W x Y x EV x (CPI^A – CPI^B)/CPI^B} – (10% x W x Y x EV) = L

PROVIDED THAT if L under Formula B is less than zero for the relevant Fuel Category solely as a result of the deduction of the ten percent (10%), the adjustment for that Fuel Category shall be zero.

where:

CPIA = the Consumer Price Index for the Adjustment Month, subject to sub-clause PV2.5.

CPIB = the Consumer Price Index for the Base Month.

Appendix 4 to Clause PV2

EXCEPTIONAL INCREASES UNDER SUB-CLAUSE PV2.8.4

Part I: Materials

Exceptional increases arise only when F2 is greater than or equal to D1 plus 50% and also greater than F1 plus 50%.

The formula for calculating exceptional increases in respect of any Material Category pursuant to sub-clause PV2.8.4 is:

$$\{W \times Y \times Z \times P \times (F2 - F1)/F1\} - (50\% \times W \times Y \times Z \times P) = M$$

where:

W = W as defined in Appendix 2.

Y = Y as defined in Appendix 2.

Z = Z as defined in Appendix 2.

P = P as defined in Appendix 2.

D1 = The Index Figure corresponding to the relevant Material Category at the Designated Date or, if a Recovery Date has been agreed or determined, at the Recovery Date.

F1 = The Index Figure corresponding to the relevant Material Category in the month preceding the month during which the middle day of the period during which the works occurred that correspond to the relevant Interim Certificate or the Final Certificate falls **provided however** that if the Date for Substantial Completion of the Works or a relevant Section falls in or after this month there shall be no adjustment to the Contract Sum.

F2 = The Index Figure for the relevant Material Category applicable at the middle day of the period during which the works occurred that correspond to the relevant Interim Certificate or the Final Certificate, **provided however** that if any Certificate is calculated in respect of a period that includes works after the Date for Substantial Completion of the Works or a relevant Section, then the Index Figure in respect of the works after relevant Date for Substantial Completion shall be the Index Figure for that Material Category at that Date for Substantial Completion.

M = The amount of the increase recoverable under sub-clause PV2.8.4 in respect of a particular Material Category in an Interim or Final Certificate.

Part II: Fuel

Exceptional increases arise only when F1 is greater than or equal to D1 plus 50% and also greater than F1 plus 50%.

The formula for calculating exceptional increases in respect of any Fuel Category pursuant to sub-clause PV2.8.4 is:

$$\{W \times Y \times EV \times (F2 - F1)/F1\} - (50\% \times W \times Y \times EV) = N$$

where:

W = W as defined in Appendix 3.

Y = Y as defined in Appendix 3.

EV = EV as defined in Appendix 3.

D1 = The Index Figure corresponding to the relevant Fuel Category at the Designated Date or, if a Recovery Date has been agreed or determined, at the Recovery Date.

F1 = The Index Figure corresponding to the relevant Fuel Category in the month preceding the month in which the middle day of the period during which the works occurred that correspond to the relevant Interim Certificate or the Final Certificate falls **provided however** that if the Date for Substantial Completion of the Works or a relevant Section falls in or after this month there shall be no adjustment to the Contract Sum.

F2 = The Index Figure for the relevant Fuel Category applicable at the middle day of the period during which the works occurred that correspond to the relevant Interim Certificate or the Final Certificate, **provided however** that if any Certificate is calculated in respect of a period that includes works after the Date for Substantial Completion of the Works or a relevant Section, then the Index Figure in respect of the works after the relevant Date for Substantial Completion shall be the Index Figure for that Fuel Category at that Date for Substantial Completion.

N = The amount of the exceptional increase recoverable under sub-clause PV2.8.4 in respect of a particular Fuel Category in an Interim or Final Certificate.

Appendix 5 to Clause PV2

NON-REUSABLE TEMPORARY WORKS

The formulae for price fluctuations in Non-Reusable Temporary Works are as follows:

A. ***Formula to be used where CPIA – CPIB is less than or equal to zero:***

$$Y \text{ x } Z \text{ x } P \text{ x } (CPI^{A} - CPI^{B})/CPI^{B} = K$$

B. ***Formula to be used where CPIA – CPIB is greater than zero:***

$$\{Y \text{ x } Z \text{ x } P \text{ x } (CPI^{A} - CPI^{B})/CPI^{B}\} - (10\% \text{ x } Y \text{ x } Z \text{ x } P) = K$$

PROVIDED THAT if K under Formula B is less than zero for Non-Reusable Temporary Works solely as a result of the deduction of the ten percent (10%), the adjustment for Non-Reusable Temporary Works shall be zero.

(Note: Formula B will deduct 10% from any increase in the indices and effectively sets Base Index + 10% as the threshold at which recovery starts.)

where:

Y = The Non-Reusable Temporary Works Percentage.

Z = Z as defined in Appendix 2.

P = The amount which is due in any Interim or Final Certificate for Non-Reusable Temporary Works less the last amount, if any, for Non-Reusable Temporary Works included in an Interim Certificate with the resulting balance divided by the total amount for Non-Reusable Temporary Works in the Contract Sum provided the aggregate value of P in respect of any Non-Reusable Temporary Works calculated over the course of the contract shall not exceed 1. In the calculation of "P" all amounts relating to the recovery of price adjustments shall be excluded.

The amounts in the Interim Certificates and/or Final Certificate used to calculate this proportion "P" are those for Work Elements allocated to Non-Reusable Temporary Works in the Pricing Document or other pricing document forming part of the Contract.

No amount for a Work Element (or part of a Work Element) in the Pricing Document, or other pricing document forming part of the Contract may be used for the calculation of adjustments for more than one Category.

CPIA = The Consumer Price Index for the Adjustment Month, subject to sub-clause PV2.5.

CPIB = The Consumer Price Index for the Base Month.

K = The amount of increase or decrease recoverable.

Appendix 6 to Clause PV2

LABOUR

The formula for Labour Variations (LV) pursuant to sub-clause PV2.8.6 is:

$$LV = Y \times GRI \times EV$$

where:

LV = The amount of increase or decrease recoverable in respect of Labour in an Interim or Final Certificate.

Y = The Labour Percentage.

GRI = The currently applicable General Round Increase expressed as a percentage. Only General Round Increases coming into effect after the Base Date and prior to the Date for Substantial Completion of the Works or a relevant Section shall be applicable. Where there are two or more General Round Increases that apply concurrently, the average General Round Increase shall apply.

General Round Increases exclude any increase in workers' wages that exceeds the percentage increases in basic pay in the private sector as agreed in the current Social Partnership Agreement.

EV = Effective Value (excluding VAT).

Provided however that if there is no Social Partnership Agreement or government guidelines in effect during the relevant Adjustment Period the following formula shall apply for calculating Labour Variations in lieu of General Round Increases:

$$LV = (CPI^{\mathbf{A}} - CPI^{\mathbf{B}})/CPI^{\mathbf{B}} \times Y \times EV$$

where:

CPIA = The Consumer Price Index for the Adjustment Month, subject to sub-clause PV2.5.

CPIB = The Consumer Price Index for the Base Month.

MODEL FORMS

CONTENTS

MODEL FORM 1.1

Bid Bond[1]

To:	*The **Employer***	
	Address of Employer	
Date:		

Regarding:	*The Contract*	
and	*The **Tenderer***	
	Address of Tenderer	

From:	*The **Surety***	
	Address of Surety	

The Tenderer proposes to submit a tender to you for the above contract. It is a requirement for submitting the tender that a bond, in these terms and in the amount of 10%[2] of the amount of the tendered contract sum, be submitted with the tender.

BY THIS BID BOND, we, the Surety, guarantee to you that, if you accept the above tender, the Tenderer will, within the time required by the contract formed by that acceptance, execute under seal and deliver the Agreement referred to in that contract and give you the fully executed and delivered performance bond and other documents required under clause 9.1 of the Conditions of that contract, all in compliance with the contract. If the Tenderer fails to do so, or otherwise repudiates its tender, we will, subject to this bond, pay all the loss you sustain as a result, up to the maximum of €0.

This bond will expire on [3] when we will be released of liability under it, unless you have before that date notified us that the Tenderer has defaulted in any of the obligations guaranteed by this bond.

We will not be released in any way or discharged by time, indulgence, waiver, alteration, release or compromise or any other circumstances that might operate as a release of a guarantor at law or in equity.

This bond is governed by and construed according to Irish law and we submit to the jurisdiction of the Irish courts to determine all matters concerning it.

We appoint as our agent for the service of legal proceedings:

Name of Agent	
Address of Agent	

We confirm that the named agent has been irrevocably appointed and the agent's failure to notify us of receipt of a document will not invalidate any proceedings or the service of the document[4].

---

[1] If the Surety is not incorporated in Ireland, execution will be in accordance with the law of its jurisdiction of incorporation for execution in Ireland.

[2] If not otherwise specified, read as 10%

[3] Date to be inserted which is 120 days after the last date for receipt of tender

[4] An address in Ireland is required when the Surety does not have a registered office in Ireland.

Given under the common seal of

Name of Surety	
Affix common seal	
Signatures of persons authorised to authenticate the seal	

OR

Signed, sealed and delivered by

Name of attorney	
Signature of attorney	
As lawful attorney of the Surety under a power of attorney dated	
Affix attorney's personal seal	

In the presence of

Name of witness	
Signature of witness	
Witness's occupation	
Witness's address	

Note

This is a model form of the bid bond that may be used with a Public Works Contract. A bid bond is effectively a contract of guarantee whereby the guarantor or surety (authorised to do guarantee business) undertakes to pay damages to a second party, in this case the Employer, when the Contractor does not honour his tender. In essence, the guarantor undertakes to be answerable for losses suffered by the Employer if the Contractor withdraws following a bid.

MODEL FORM 1.2

Letters Notifying Candidates/Tenderers

For the Open Procedure above the threshold of €5.20 million a number of letters are used to notify Tenderers at appropriate stages. These are:

1 – Letter to a Tenderer eliminating them from the Tender competition on the basis that they have submitted a non-compliant Tender

2 – Letter to a Tenderer who has submitted an apparently Abnormally Low Tender requesting them to submit details of various aspects of their Tender

3 – Letter to a Tenderer eliminating them from the Tender competition on the basis that they have been deemed by the Contracting Authority to have submitted an ALT.

This letter may only be sent after the Contracting Authority has considered the constituent elements of the Tender

4 – Letter to a Tenderer who has been identified as the Lowest Price/Most Economically Advantageous Tender requesting them to submit evidence in support of qualification criteria that they have declared to have met in their Tender submission

5 – Letter to a Tenderer eliminating them from the Tender competition on the basis that their documentary evidence failed to verify that they meet the pre-qualification criteria they declared to have met in their Tender submission

6 – Letter to the Successful Tenderer

This letter must be sent by the Contracting Authority at the same time as the Letter to Unsuccessful Tenderers for the Standstill Period to be valid.

7 – Letter to Unsuccessful Tenderer(s)

This letter must be sent by the Contracting Authority at the same time as the Letter to Successful Tenderer for the Standstill Period to be valid.

8 – Letter to non-compliant/Eliminated Tenderers where a period of 30 days has not elapsed between the letter notifying them of their non-compliance/elimination and the date that the letters are sent to Successful and Unsuccessful Tenderers

This letter must be sent by the Contracting Authority at the same time as the Letter to Successful Tenderer and the Letter to Unsuccessful Tenderers for the Standstill Period to be valid.

Frameworks

Letters notifying tenderers that they have been awarded a place on a framework should follow the format of the Letter to Successful Tenderer, however Contracting Authorities must have regard to the call-off rules for the framework in question and additional information may be appropriate in certain cases. For example it may be appropriate to advise tenderers of their scores relative to the first ranked tenderer where the call off rules are based on rankings.

MODEL FORM 1.3

NOTE:
Model Form 1.3 has been withdrawn and has been replaced by MF1.2 Letters Notifying Candidates/ Tenderers.

MODEL FORM 1.4

Letter of Acceptance

Note Please click + left of title 'Letter of Acceptance' to read Employers Instructions prior to issue of letter.

To:	*[Name and address of tenderer]*
Regarding:	*[Name of contract]*
Date:	

A Dhaoine Uaisle
I refer to your tender for the above Contract dated [1] (the **Tender**). Terms used in this letter that are defined in the Conditions of that Contract have the same meaning in this letter.

On the basis that the contract formed by acceptance of your Tender will consist of the documents set out below, I accept your Tender:

- This Letter of Acceptance
- The Agreement
- The Conditions of *[insert full name of selected contract form*]
- The Tender and Schedule appended[2] to this Letter of Acceptance
- Any Novated Design Documents
- The following post-tender clarifications[3]:

This is the Letter of Acceptance referred to in the Conditions.

The Contract Sum is euro [excluding VAT/ including VAT at standard and zero rates only/ including VAT at standard, reduced and zero rates].[4]

I draw attention to your obligations in clause 9.1 of the Conditions about documents to be provided before the Starting Date.

Please return to me a copy of this letter acknowledging receipt as indicated below.

Is mise, le meas

Signed ____________________________
On behalf of *[Name of Employer]*, duly authorised to accept the Tender

---

ACKNOWLEDGEMENT

[1] Insert date of tender
[2] Ensure that Schedule is appended to the letter
[3] Insert references to any post-tender clarifications
[4] Keep the one that is relevant and delete the other two.

We acknowledge receipt of this letter on ___________ (date).

Signed ______________________________
On behalf of *[Name of the Contractor]*

MODEL FORM 1.5

Letter to Tenderers Notifying Award

To:	*[Name and address of tenderer]*
Regarding:	*[name of contract]*
Date:	

A Dhaoine Uaisle

I write to inform you that the above contract has been awarded to *[name of winning tenderer]*.

I would like to thank you again for the interest you have shown in this competition.

Please acknowledge receipt of this letter by signing the acknowledgement below and returning to me.

Is mise, le meas

Signed: ....

On behalf of *[Name of Employer]*

ACKNOWLEDGEMENT

We acknowledge receipt of this letter on ___________ (date).

Signed ____________________________

On behalf of *[Name of the unsuccessful Tenderer]*

Note
This is a model of the letter sent by the Client/Employer to the unsuccessful Tenderers after the Contract has been awarded.

MODEL FORM 1.6

Performance Bond[1]

(Clause 1.5)

Bond No. [ ] BONDAMOUNT: € [ ]

THIS BOND is made on [ ] **BETWEEN**

1.	*The* ***Contractor***	
	Registered office of Contractor	
2.	*The* ***Surety***	
	Registered office of Surety	
and		
3.	*The* ***Employer***	
	Principal office of Employer	

BACKGROUND

A. The Employer and the Contractor have or will enter into a contract for

Description of Works [ ]

(the **Contract**).

B. The Contractor has agreed to furnish a performance bond to the Employer.

C. Terms defined in the Contract have the same meaning in this Bond.

IT IS AGREED AS FOLLOWS:

1. If the Contractor's obligation to complete the Works is terminated under clause 12.1 of the Conditions the Surety will, subject to this Bond, pay the Employer any amount for which the Contractor is liable under clause 12.2.11 of the Conditions.

2. If the Contractor breaches the Contract the Surety will, subject to this Bond, pay the Employer any amount for which the Contractor is liable to the Employer as damages for breach of the Contract, as established under the Contract, taking into account all sums due to the Contractor under the Contract.

3. The liability of the Surety under this Bond will not exceed € [ ]. This amount will be reduced by half on issue of the Certificate of Substantial Completion of the Works under the Contract.

4. No alteration in the Contract or in the extent or nature of the works to be done under it, and no allowance of time under the Contract, and no forbearance or forgiveness concerning the Contract by the Employer, will in any way release the Surety from liability under this Bond.

5. The Surety will be released from its liability under this Bond [450] days[2] after the certificate of Substantial Completion of the Works has been issued, except in relation to any breach by the Contractor or termination that has occurred before that date, written notice (including particulars of the breach or termination) of which has been given to the Surety earlier than 4 weeks after this expiry date.

---

[1] If the Contractor and/or Surety is/are not incorporated in Ireland, execution will be in accordance with the law of its jurisdiction of incorporation for execution in Ireland.

[2] If not otherwise specified, read as 450 days.

6. The Contractor undertakes to the Surety to perform its obligations under the Contract. This undertaking does not limit any rights or remedies of the Employer or the Surety.

7. The Employer may, but is not required to, provide to the Surety a copy of any notice that the Employer gives to or receives from the Contractor under clause 12 of the Conditions.

8. The decision of a court or arbitrator in a dispute between the Employer and the Contractor will be binding on the Surety as to all matters concerning a breach of the Contract, termination under the Contract, and the Contractor's liability.

9. If the Surety is called on to pay the Employer's loss following a termination under clause 12.1 of the Conditions, the Surety may suggest a completion contractor to the Employer, provided the proposed completion contractor is acceptable to the Employer.

10. The Surety will not be liable under this Bond for a breach or termination caused solely and directly by war, invasion, act of foreign enemies, hostilities (whether war is declared or not), terrorism, civil war, rebellion, revolution, or military or usurped power.

11. The Employer may assign the benefit of this Bond, without the Surety's or the Contractor's consent, by giving written notice to the Surety.

12. This Bond is governed by and construed according to Irish law and the parties submit to the jurisdiction of the Irish courts to determine all matters concerning it.

13. Money payable by the Surety under this Bond will be paid in euro in Ireland.

14. The Surety appoints

Name of Agent:

Address of Agent:

as its agent for service of legal proceedings. The Surety confirms that the named agent has been irrevocably appointed and the failure of the agent to notify the Surety of receipt of a document will not invalidate any proceedings or the service of the document.[4]

Given[3] under the Contractor's common seal

Affix Contractor's common seal	
Signatures of persons authorised to authenticate the seal	

OR

Signed, sealed and delivered by

Name of attorney	
Signature of attorney	
As lawful attorney of the Contractor under a power of attorney dated	
Affix attorney's personal seal	

In the presence of

---

[3] If the Contractor and/or Surety is/are not incorporated in Ireland, execution will be in accordance with the law of its jurisdiction of incorporation for execution in Ireland.

[4] An address in Ireland is required when the Surety does not have a registered office in Ireland.

Name of witness	
Signature of witness	
Witness's occupation	
Witness's address	

OR

Signed on behalf of

Name of Contractor	
Signature of authorised person	

In the presence of

Name of witness	
Signature of witness	
Witness's occupation	
Witness's address	

OR (if the Contractor is an individual)

Signed, sealed and delivered by

Name of Contractor	
Signature of Contractor	
Affix personal seal	

In the presence of

Signature of witness	
Name of witness	
Witness's occupation	
Witness's address	

OR

Signed by

____

Name of Contractor	
Signature of Contractor	

In the presence of

Name of witness	
Signature of witness	
Witness's occupation	
Witness's address	

OR (if the Contractor is a joint venture, execution must be by each member, using the blocks below)

Joint Venture Member 1

Given under the common seal of

Name of joint venture member 1	
Affix common seal	
Signatures of persons authorised to authenticate the seal	

OR

Signed, sealed and delivered by

Name of attorney	
Signature of attorney	
As lawful attorney of joint venture member 1 under a power of attorney dated	
Affix attorney's personal seal	

In the presence of

Name of witness	
Signature of witness	
Witness's occupation	
Witness's address	

OR

Signed on behalf of

Name of joint venture member 1	
Signature of authorised person	

In the presence of

Name of witness	
Signature of witness	
Witness's occupation	
Witness's address	

Joint Venture Member 2

Given under the common seal of

Name of joint venture member 2	
Affix common seal	
Signatures of persons authorised to authenticate the seal	

OR

Signed, sealed and delivered by

Name of attorney	
Signature of attorney	
As lawful attorney of joint venture member 2 under a power of attorney dated	
Affix attorney's personal seal	

In the presence of

Name of witness	
Signature of witness	
Witness's occupation	
Witness's address	

OR

Signed on behalf of

Name of joint venture member 2	
Signature of authorised person	

In the presence of

Name of witness	
Signature of witness	
Witness's occupation	
Witness's address	

Joint Venture Member 3

Given under the common seal of

Name of joint venture member 3	
Affix common seal	
Signatures of persons authorised to authenticate the seal	

OR

Signed, sealed and delivered by

Name of attorney	
Signature of attorney	
As lawful attorney of joint venture member 3 under a power of attorney dated	
Affix attorney's personal seal	

In the presence of

Name of witness	
Signature of witness	
Witness's occupation	
Witness's address	

OR

Signed on behalf of

Name of joint venture member 3	
Signature of authorised person	

In the presence of

Name of witness	
Signature of witness	
Witness's occupation	
Witness's address	

Given under the Surety's common seal

Affix Surety's common seal	
Signatures of persons authorised to authenticate the seal	

OR

Signed, sealed and delivered by

Name of attorney	
Signature of attorney	
As lawful attorney of the Surety under a power of attorney dated	
Affix attorney's personal seal	

In the presence of

Name of witness	
Signature of witness	
Witness's occupation	
Witness's address	

Note

This is a model of the performance bond that may be used with a Public Works Contract. A Performance Bond is effectively a contract of guarantee whereby the guarantor or surety (authorised to do guarantee business) undertakes to pay damages to a second party, in this case the Employer, arising from a breach of contract, for losses sustained by the Employer due to non-performance by the Contractor.

MODEL FORM 1.7

Parent Company Guarantee[1]

(Clause 1.6)

THIS GUARANTEE is made on [ ] **BETWEEN**

1.	*The* ***Contractor***	
	Registered office of Contractor	
2.	*The* ***Guarantor***	
	Registered office of Guarantor	

and

3.	*The* ***Employer***	
	Whose principal office is at	

BACKGROUND

A. The Employer and the Contractor have or will enter into a contract for

Description of Works [ ]

(the **Contract**).

B. The Guarantor has agreed to guarantee the Contractor's performance of the Contract.

C. Terms defined in the Contract have the same meaning in this Guarantee.

IT IS AGREED AS FOLLOWS:

1 Guarantee

The Guarantor irrevocably and unconditionally:

1.1 guarantees to the Employer that the Contractor will punctually perform all its obligations under the Contract and

1.2 undertakes to the Employer to fully perform the Contractor's obligations under the Contract if the Contractor fails to perform them.

2 Indemnity

If the Contractor's obligations under the Contract or the Guarantor's obligations under clause 1 above are or become void or unenforceable then, as between the Guarantor and the Employer (but without affecting the Contractor's obligations), the Guarantor will as principal obligor indemnify the Employer against any resulting loss and be liable to the Employer for the same amount as the Guarantor would have been liable for if the obligations had not been void or unenforceable.

3 Contractor's failure to perform

3.1 If the Contractor goes into liquidation, administration, examinership or receivership or becomes subject to any other form of insolvency proceedings, or if the Contractor's obligation to complete the Works is lawfully terminated under sub-clause 12.1 of the Conditions of the Contract, any such event will be conclusive evidence, for the purposes of this Guarantee, that the Contractor has failed to perform the Contract.

3.2 The decision of a court or arbitrator or an agreement between the Contractor and the Employer will be binding on the Guarantor in relation to any failure by the Contractor to perform the Contract.

---

[1] If the Contractor and/or the Guarantors is/are not incorporated in Ireland, execution will be in accordance with the law of its jurisdiction of incorporation for execution in Ireland.

4. Guarantee is in addition to other security
The Guarantor's obligations are in addition to and independent of any other security the Employer may at any time hold for the Contractor's obligations under the Contract.

5. Continuing guarantee
The Guarantor's liability will continue until the Contractor has performed all its obligations in full, and will not be satisfied or diminished by any payment or recovery of an amount due from the Contractor to the Employer.

6. Guarantor's liability not impaired
The Guarantor's liability under this Guarantee is as principal obligor and not merely as surety. Neither the Guarantor's liability under this Guarantee nor the Employer's rights under it will be affected by any of the following, whether or not known to any of the parties:

6.1 the Contractor's obligations under the Contract being or becoming illegal, invalid or unenforceable, if it would not be illegal for the Guarantor to fulfil the obligation

6.2 bankruptcy, insolvency, liquidation, examinership, dissolution, amalgamation, winding up, reorganisation or any similar proceeding concerning the Contractor

6.3 change in the status, function, control or ownership of the Contractor

6.4 death or incapacity of the Contractor

6.5 amendment to the Contract or change to the works to be done under it (whether or not the amendment or change increases the Guarantor's liability)

6.6 time being given to the Contractor

6.7 a concession, arrangement, waiver or other indulgence being granted or made or agreed to be granted or made by the Employer

6.8 anything that the Employer or the Contractor do or fail to do, including without limitation:
(1) asserting or pursuing (or failing or delaying to assert, perfect or enforce) rights or remedies or
(2) giving security or releasing, modifying, or exchanging security or
(3) having or incurring any liability

6.9 assignment of the benefit of the Contract

6.10 whole or partial discharge (whether of the Contractor's obligations or security for them or otherwise) or arrangement made on the faith of payment, security or other disposition that is avoided or must be repaid on bankruptcy, liquidation or otherwise

6.11 rights against third parties that the Employer may have relating to performance of the Contractor's obligations

6.12 a reduction in, or other arrangement relating to, the Contractor's liability to the Employer as a result of an arrangement or composition under the Companies (Amendment) Act, 1990 or any similar provision

6.13 any other act, event, fact, circumstance, rule of law, or omission.

7. Guarantor not to claim against or in competition with the Employer
For as long as the Contractor has actual or contingent obligations or liability under the Contract, the Guarantor shall not:

7.1 be entitled to share in the Employer's rights under the Contract or any other rights or security of the Employer or

7.2 in competition with the Employer, seek to enforce any rights concerning the Guarantor performing or having obligations under this Guarantee

and if the Guarantor receives money from the Contractor in relation to a payment of the Guarantor under this Guarantee, the Guarantor will hold the money in trust for the Employer as long as the Guarantor has any liability (contingent or otherwise) under this Guarantee.

8. No preconditions upon Employer
The Employer may enforce this Guarantee without exercising rights against the Contractor or anyone else.

9. Assignment
The Employer may assign the benefit of this Guarantee without the Guarantor's or Contractor's consent. The Employer shall give notice to the Guarantor within 28 days after any assignment.

10. Partial invalidity
If at any time any part of this Guarantee is or becomes illegal, invalid or unenforceable, the rest of this Guarantee will remain legal, valid and enforceable.

11. Law and Jurisdiction
This Guarantee is governed by and construed according to Irish law and the parties submit to the jurisdiction of the Irish courts to determine all matters concerning it.

12. Notices
Any communication given in connection with this Guarantee must be in writing and delivered to, or sent by pre-paid registered post to the relevant party's address at the top of this Guarantee, or the Guarantor's agent's address in clause 13 below, or another address notified in writing by the relevant party. Pre-paid registered post is taken to have been received 2 days after it was sent.

13. Agent for Service[2]
The Guarantor appoints

Name of Agent	
Address of Agent	

as its agent for service of legal proceedings. The Guarantor confirms that the named agent has been irrevocably appointed and the failure of the agent to notify the Guarantor of receipt of a document will not invalidate any proceedings or the service of the document.

14. Representations and Warranties
The Guarantor represents and warrants to the Employer that:

14.1 the execution, delivery and performance of this Guarantee by the Guarantor has been duly and validly authorised by all requisite corporate action by the Guarantor and

14.2 this Guarantee is the Guarantor's legal, valid and binding obligation in accordance with its terms and

14.3 no approval or consent from any governmental entity or any other person or entity is required in connection with the execution, delivery or performance of this Guarantee by the Guarantor.

Given[3] under the Guarantor's common seal

Affix Guarantor's common seal	
Signatures of persons authorised to authenticate the seal	

OR

Signed, sealed and delivered by

Name of attorney	
Signature of attorney	
As lawful attorney of the Guarantor under a power of attorney dated	
Affix attorney's personal seal	

2 An address in Ireland is required when the Guarantor does not have a registered office in Ireland.

3 If the Contractor and/or Guarantor is/are not incorporated in Ireland, execution will be in accordance with the law of its jurisdiction of incorporation for execution in Ireland.

In the presence of

Name of witness	
Signature of witness	
Witness's occupation	
Witness's address	

Given under the Contractor's common seal

Affix Contractor's common seal	
Signatures of persons authorised to authenticate the seal	

OR

Signed, sealed and delivered by

Name of attorney	
Signature of attorney	
As lawful attorney of the Contractor under a power of attorney dated	
Affix attorney's personal seal	

In the presence of

Name of witness	
Signature of witness	
Witness's occupation	
Witness's address	

OR

Signed on behalf of

Name of Contractor	
Signature of authorised person	

In the presence of

Name of witness	
Signature of witness	
Witness's occupation	
Witness's address	

OR (if the Contractor is an individual)

Signed, sealed and delivered by

Name of Contractor	
Signature of Contractor	
Affix personal seal	

In the presence of

Signature of witness	
Name of witness	
Witness's occupation	
Witness's address	

OR

Signed by

Name of Contractor	
Signature of Contractor	

In the presence of

Name of witness	
Signature of witness	
Witness's occupation	
Witness's address	

OR (if the Contractor is a joint venture, execution must be by each member, using the blocks below)

Joint Venture Member 1

Given under the common seal of

Name of joint venture member 1	
Affix common seal	
Signatures of persons authorised to authenticate the seal	

OR

Signed, sealed and delivered by

Name of attorney	
Signature of attorney	
As lawful attorney of joint venture member 1 under a power of attorney dated	
Affix attorney's personal seal	

In the presence of

Name of witness	
Signature of witness	
Witness's occupation	
Witness's address	

OR

Signed on behalf of

Name of joint venture member 1	
Signature of authorised person	

In the presence of

Name of witness	
Signature of witness	
Witness's occupation	
Witness's address	

Joint Venture Member 2

Given under the common seal of

Name of joint venture member 2	
Affix common seal	
Signatures of persons authorised to authenticate the seal	

OR

Signed, sealed and delivered by

Name of attorney	
Signature of attorney	
As lawful attorney of joint venture member 2 under a power of attorney dated	
Affix attorney's personal seal	

In the presence of

Name of witness	
Signature of witness	
Witness's occupation	
Witness's address	

OR

Signed on behalf of

Name of joint venture member 2	
Signature of authorised person	

In the presence of

Name of witness	
Signature of witness	
Witness's occupation	
Witness's address	

Joint Venture Member 3

Given under the common seal of

Name of joint venture member 3	
Affix common seal	
Signatures of persons authorised to authenticate the seal	

OR

Signed, sealed and delivered by

Name of attorney	
Signature of attorney	
As lawful attorney of joint venture member 3 under a power of attorney dated	
Affix attorney's personal seal	

In the presence of

Name of witness	
Signature of witness	
Witness's occupation	
Witness's address	

OR

Signed on behalf of

Name of joint venture member 3	
Signature of authorised person	

In the presence of

Name of witness	
Signature of witness	
Witness's occupation	
Witness's address	

Note
This is a model of the parent company guarantee that may be used with a Public Works Contract. A parent company guarantee assures the Employer recourse to the parent company's financial standing, technical capability and resources provided the parent company is prepared to underwrite the liabilities of its subsidiary in the competition.

MODEL FORM 1.8

Novation and Guarantee Agreement[1]

(To be used when the Contract is to be novated to a joint venture company)

THIS AGREEMENT is made on

BETWEEN

1.	*The **Contractor***		
	Registered office of Contractor		
2.	*Name of Guarantor 1*	*Name of Guarantor 2*	*Name of Guarantor 3*
	(hereinafter together referred to as the **Guarantors**)		
	Registered office of Guarantor 1	*Registered office of Guarantor 2*	*Registered office of Guarantor 3*

and

3.	*The **Employer***	
	Whose principal office is at	

BACKGROUND

A. The Employer and the Guarantors have entered or will enter into a contract for

Description of Works	

(the **Contract**).

B. The Guarantors have formed the Contractor as their subsidiary for the purpose of completing the Contract.

C. This Agreement is for the Contract to be novated from the Employer and the Guarantors to the Employer and the Contractor, and for the Guarantors jointly and severally to guarantee the Contractor's performance of the Contract.

D. Terms defined in the Contract have the same meaning in this Agreement.

IT IS AGREED AS FOLLOWS:

1 No amount due
The Guarantors acknowledge that no amount is due to them under the Contract on the date of this Agreement.

2 Novation
The Contract is novated from the Employer of the one part and the Guarantors of the other to the Employer of the one part and the Contractor of the other.

3 Contract affirmed

3.1 Subject to this Agreement, the Contract remains in effect.

3.2 The Contractor is bound and treated as if always bound to perform the Contractor's obligations and

---

[1] If the Contractor and/or the Guarantors is/are not incorporated in Ireland, execution will be in accordance with the law of its jurisdiction of incorporation for execution in Ireland.

observe the Contract as if the Contractor were and always had been named as "the Contractor" in the Contract in place of the Guarantors.

3.3 The Employer is bound and treated as if always bound to perform the Employer's obligations and observe the Contract for the benefit of the Contractor as if the Contractor were and always had been named as "the Contractor" in the Contract in place of the Guarantors.

4 Warranty

The Guarantors and the Contractor represent and warrant to the Employer that the Contractor's duties and obligations under the Contract have been performed in accordance with the Contract.

5. Guarantee

The Guarantors irrevocably and unconditionally:

5.1 guarantee to the Employer that the Contractor will punctually perform all its obligations under the Contract and

5.2 undertake to the Employer to fully perform the Contractor's obligations under the Contract if the Contractor fails to perform them

6 Indemnity

If the Contractor's obligations under the Contract or the Guarantor's obligations under clause 5 above are or become void or unenforceable then, as between the Guarantor and the Employer (but without affecting the Contractor's obligations), the Guarantor will as principal obligor indemnify the Employer against any resulting loss and be liable to the Employer for the same amount as the Guarantor would have been liable for if the obligations had not been void or unenforceable.

7 Contractor's failure to perform

7.1 If the Contractor goes into liquidation, administration, examinership or receivership or becomes subject to any other form of insolvency proceedings, or if the Contractor's obligation to complete the Works is lawfully terminated under sub-clause 12.1 of the Conditions of the Contract, any such event will be conclusive evidence, for the purposes of this Agreement, that the Contractor has failed to perform the Contract.

7.2 The decision of a court or arbitrator or an agreement between the Contractor and the Employer will be binding on the Guarantors in relation to any failure by the Contractor to perform the Contract.

8 Guarantee is in addition to other security

The Guarantors' obligations are in addition to and independent of any other security the Employer may at any time hold for the Contractor's obligations under the Contract.

9 Continuing guarantee

The Guarantors' liability will continue until the Contractor has performed all its obligations in full, and will not be satisfied or diminished by any payment or recovery of an amount due from the Contractor to the Employer.

10 Joint and several liability

The Guarantors' liability under this Agreement is joint and several.

11 Guarantor's liability not impaired

The Guarantor's liability under this Guarantee is as principal obligor and not merely as surety. Neither the Guarantors' liability under this Agreement nor the Employer's rights under it will be affected by any of the following, whether or not known to any of the parties:

11.1 the Contractor's obligations under the Contract being or becoming illegal, invalid or unenforceable, if it would not be illegal for the Guarantor to fulfil the obligation

11.2 bankruptcy, insolvency, liquidation, examinership, dissolution, amalgamation, winding up, reorganisation or any similar proceeding concerning the Contractor

11.3 change in the status, function, control or ownership of the Contractor

11.4 death or incapacity of the Contractor

11.5 amendment to the Contract or change to the works to be done under it (whether or not the amendment or change increases the Guarantors' liability)

11.6 time being given to the Contractor

11.7 a concession, arrangement, waiver or other indulgence being granted or made or agreed to be granted or made by the Employer

11.8 anything that the Employer or the Contractor do or fail to do, including without limitation:
(1) asserting or pursuing (or failing or delaying to assert, perfect or enforce) rights or remedies or
(2) giving security or releasing, modifying, or exchanging security or
(3) having or incurring any liability

11.9 assignment of the benefit of the Contract

11.10 whole or partial discharge (whether of the Contractor's obligations or security for them or otherwise) or arrangement made on the faith of payment, security or other disposition that is avoided or must be repaid on bankruptcy, liquidation or otherwise

11.11 rights against third parties that the Employer may have relating to performance of the Contractor's obligations

11.12 a reduction in, or other arrangement relating to, the Contractor's liability to the Employer as a result of an arrangement or composition under the Companies (Amendment) Act, 1990 or any similar provision

11.13 any other act, event, fact, circumstance, rule of law, or omission.

12 Guarantors not to claim against or in competition with the Employer

For as long as the Contractor has actual or contingent obligations or liability under the Contract, the Guarantors shall not:

12.1 be entitled to share in the Employer's rights under the Contract or any other rights or security of the Employer or

12.2 in competition with the Employer, seek to enforce any rights concerning the Guarantor performing or having obligations under this Agreement

and if a Guarantor receives money from the Contractor in relation to a payment of the Guarantor under this Guarantee, the Guarantor will hold the money in trust for the Employer as long as the Guarantor has any liability (contingent or otherwise) under this Guarantee.

13 No preconditions upon Employer

The Employer may enforce this Agreement without exercising rights against the Contractor or anyone else.

14 Assignment

The Employer may assign the benefit of this Guarantee without the Guarantors' or Contractor's consent. The Employer shall give notice to the Guarantor within 28 days after any assignment.

15 Partial invalidity

If at any time any part of this Agreement is or becomes illegal, invalid or unenforceable, the rest of this Guarantee will remain legal, valid and enforceable.

16 Law and Jurisdiction

This Agreement is governed by and construed according to Irish law and the parties submit to the jurisdiction of the Irish courts to determine all matters concerning it.

17 Notices

Any communication given in connection with this Agreement must be in writing and delivered to, or sent by pre-paid registered post to the relevant party's address at the top of this Guarantee, or a Guarantor's agent's address in clause 18 below, or another address notified in writing by the relevant party. Pre-paid registered post is taken to have been received 2 days after it was sent.

18 Agent for Service[2]

The Guarantors appoint

Name of Agent	
Address of Agent	

as their agent for service of legal proceedings. The Guarantors confirm that the named agent has been irrevocably appointed and the failure of the agent to notify the Guarantors of receipt of a document will not invalidate any proceedings or the service of the document.

[2] An address in Ireland is required when none of the Guarantors has a registered office in Ireland.

19 Representations and Warranties

The Guarantors and the Contractor represent and warrant to the Employer that:

19.1 The Guarantors own the entire beneficial interest in the share capital and issued share capital of the Contractor and no-one else is entitled to appoint members of the Contractor's board of directors or to vote at meetings of the members of the Contractor.

19.2 the execution, delivery and performance of this Guarantee by the Guarantors and the Contractor has been duly and validly authorised by all requisite corporate action by the Guarantors and the Contractor and

19.3 this Agreement is the Guarantors' and the Contractor's legal, valid and binding obligation in accordance with its terms and

19.4 no approval or consent from any governmental entity or any other person or entity is required in connection with the execution, delivery or performance of this Agreement by the Guarantors or the Contractor.

Given[3] under the Guarantors' common seals

Guarantor 1

Affix Guarantor 1's seal	
Signatures of persons authorised to authenticate the seal	

Guarantor 2

Affix Guarantor 2's seal	
Signatures of persons authorised to authenticate the seal	

Guarantor 3

Affix Guarantor 3's seal	
Signatures of persons authorised to authenticate the seal	

[3] If the Contractor and/or the Guarantors is/are not incorporated in Ireland, execution will be in accordance with the law of its jurisdiction of incorporation for execution in Ireland.

Given under the Contractor's common seal

Affix Contractor's common seal	
Signatures of persons authorised to authenticate the seal	

OR

Signed, sealed and delivered by

Name of attorney	
Signature of attorney	
As lawful attorney of the Contractor under a power of attorney dated	
Affix attorney's personal seal	

In the presence of

Name of witness	
Signature of witness	
Witness's occupation	
Witness's address	

OR

Signed on behalf of

Name of Contractor	
Signature of authorised person	

In the presence of

Name of witness	
Signature of witness	
Witness's occupation	
Witness's address	

OR (if the Contractor is an individual)

Signed, sealed and delivered by

Name of Contractor	
Signature of Contractor	
Affix personal seal	

In the presence of

Signature of witness	
Name of witness	
Witness's occupation	
Witness's address	

OR

Signed by

Name of Contractor	
Signature of Contractor	

In the presence of

Name of witness	
Signature of witness	
Witness's occupation	
Witness's address	

OR (if the Contractor is a joint venture, execution must be by each member, using the blocks below)

Joint Venture Member 1

Given under the common seal of

Name of joint venture member 1	
Affix common seal	
Signatures of persons authorised to authenticate the seal	

OR

Signed, sealed and delivered by

Name of attorney	
Signature of attorney	
As lawful attorney of joint venture member 1 under a power of attorney dated	
Affix attorney's personal seal	

In the presence of

Name of witness	
Signature of witness	
Witness's occupation	
Witness's address	

OR

Signed on behalf of

Name of joint venture member 1	
Signature of authorised person	

In the presence of

Name of witness	
Signature of witness	
Witness's occupation	
Witness's address	

Joint Venture Member 2

Given under the common seal of

Name of joint venture member 2	
Affix common seal	
Signatures of persons authorised to authenticate the seal	

OR

Signed, sealed and delivered by

Name of attorney		
Signature of attorney		
As lawful attorney of joint venture member 2 under a power of attorney dated		
Affix attorney's personal seal		

In the presence of

Name of witness	
Signature of witness	
Witness's occupation	
Witness's address	

OR

Signed on behalf of

Name of joint venture member 2	
Signature of authorised person	

In the presence of

Name of witness	
Signature of witness	
Witness's occupation	
Witness's address	

Joint Venture Member 3

Given under the common seal of

Name of joint venture member	
Affix common seal	
Signatures of persons authorised to authenticate the seal	

OR

Signed, sealed and delivered by

Name of attorney		
Signature of attorney		
As lawful attorney of joint venture member 3 under a power of attorney dated		
Affix attorney's personal seal		

In the presence of

Name of witness	
Signature of witness	
Witness's occupation	
Witness's address	

OR

Signed on behalf of

Name of joint venture member 3	
Signature of authorised person	

In the presence of

Name of witness	
Signature of witness	
Witness's occupation	
Witness's address	

Given under the Employer's seal

Affix Employer's seal	
Signatures of persons authorised to authenticate the seal	

OR

Signed on behalf of the Employer

Signature of authorised person	

In the presence of

Name of witness	
Signature of witness	
Witness's occupation	
Witness's address	

Note

Novation is where the Contractor takes over the role and responsibilities of the Employer in relation to a contract that the Employer has with another party. This arises where an Employer enters into a contract with another party with the intention that at some time during that contract the main Contractor will replace the Employer through a novation arrangement. MF 1.8 is the model of the novation and guarantee agreement that may be used with a Public Works Contract where the contract is being novated to a joint venture company.

MODEL FORM 1.9

Novation Agreement[1]

(Clause 5.4 of PW-CF1 to PW-CF5)

THIS AGREEMENT is made on [ ] **BETWEEN:**

1.	*The **Main Contractor***	
	Registered office of Main Contractor	
2.	*The **Specialist***	
	Registered office of Specialist	

and

3.	*The **Employer***	
	Whose principal office is at	

BACKGROUND

A. By written agreement dated [ ] (the Specialist Contract) the Employer has appointed the Specialist to

Description of works, services or supply	

in connection with

Name of main Contract	

B. The Employer has appointed the Main Contractor to do Works, which include what the Specialist is to do under the Specialist Contract.

C. The parties to this Agreement have agreed to the novation of the Specialist Contract from the Employer and Specialist to the Main Contractor and Specialist.

D. Terms defined in the Specialist Contract have the same meaning in this Agreement.

IT IS AGREED as follows:

1. **Payment**
The Specialist confirms that all money due under the Specialist Contract to the date of this Agreement has been paid in full.

2. **Novation**
The Specialist Contract is novated from the Employer and the Specialist to the Main Contractor and the Specialist.

3. **Affirmation of Subcontract**

3.1 Subject to this Agreement, the Specialist Contract remains in effect.

---

1 ***If the Contractor and/or Guarantors is/are not incorporated in Ireland, execution will be in accordance with the law of its jurisdiction of incorporation for execution in Ireland.***

3.2 The Specialist is bound, and considered always to have been bound, to perform the Specialist's obligations for the benefit of the Main Contractor, as if the Main Contractor were and always had been named as 'the Employer' in the Specialist Contract in place of the Employer.

3.3 Similarly, the Main Contractor is bound, and considered always to have been bound, to perform the Employer's obligations for the benefit of the Specialist as if the Main Contractor were and always had been named as 'the Employer' in the Specialist Contract in place of the Employer.

4. **Amendments to Specialist Contract**
From the date of this Agreement, the Specialist Contract is amended as follows:

4.1 The person named in or under the Specialist Contract as Employer's Representative will cease to be the Employer's Representative and the Main Contractor will be the Employer's Representative under the Specialist Contract.

4.2 In sub-clause 1.1 the following additional definition is added:
Main Contract *means the contract between the Employer (as Contractor) and the Employer's employer (as Employer) under which the Employer has agreed to complete work that includes the Works. The Main Contract made the appointment referred to in recital B of the Novation Agreement among the Contractor, the Employer and the Employer's employer concerning the Contract.*

4.3 Sub-clause 3.3 is deleted and replaced with the following:

3.3 Insurance of the Works and Other Risk Items

3.3.1 The Employer shall for the benefit of itself and the Contractor keep in force in accordance with the requirements of the Main Contract a policy of insurance covering the Works and Works Items. Notwithstanding sub-clause 3.2, loss and damage to the Works and Works Items shall be at the Employer's sole risk while covered by that insurance policy.

3.3.2 The Contractor shall take out insurance on terms and with an insurer approved by the Employer (such approval not to be unreasonably withheld) of the Contractor's Things against loss and damage to their full reinstatement value.

3.3.3 The Contractor shall comply with the Employer's insurance policy covering the Works and Works Items in so far as compliance is within the Contractor's control. The Contractor shall indemnify the Contractor in relation to any act or omission on the Contractor's part which causes that insurance to become invalid or ineffective in whole or in part.

4.3.1 Clause 7 is deleted and replaced with the following:

7 The Site

7.1 Lands Made Available for the Works

Subject to any restrictions in the Works Requirements, the Employer shall from time to time make available to the Contractor the parts of the Site and means of access to the Site that are necessary for the Contractor to execute the Works in accordance with the Contract, but the Employer is not bound to give the Contractor exclusive possession or exclusive control of any part of the Site, unless expressly provided for elsewhere in the Contract.

7.2 Scaffolding

The Employer shall permit the Contractor to use for the purpose of executing and completing the Works any standing scaffolding that is from time to time provided by the Employer in connection with its performance of the Main Contract, but the Employer is not bound to provide or retain scaffolding for the Contractor's use unless otherwise stated in the Contract.

7.3 Attendances

The Employer shall provide attendances as stated in the Works Requirements. Otherwise the Contractor shall provide everything necessary for the execution of the Works. The Employer will provide all attendances required by this clause in a timely manner so as not to cause delay or disrupt progress of the Works.

7.4 Waste

The Contractor shall be responsible for and bear the cost (to the extent that this cost is not recoverable by the Employer under the Main Contract) of removing from the Site and disposing of hazardous waste (as defined by the Waste Act 1996) arising from the execution of the Works.

7.5 Security of the Site and Nuisance
The Contractor shall ensure that neither it nor the Contractor's Personnel cause the Contractor to be in breach of sub-clause 7.7 (Security of the Site and Nuisance) of the Conditions of the Main Contract.

7.6 *(Not used)*

7.7 Setting out the Works
Unless otherwise agreed between the parties, the Contractor shall set out the Works in compliance with sub-clause 7.7 (Setting Out the Works) of the Main Contract.

7.8 Archaeological Object and Human Remains
If any fossils, coins, antiquities, monuments or other items of value or of archaeological or geological interest or human remains are discovered on or adjacent to the Site, unless the Works Requirements say otherwise, the Contractor shall not disturb them, but shall take all necessary steps to preserve them, and shall promptly notify the Employer [and comply with any instructions]. As between the parties, these items shall be the Employer's property.

7.9 Access and Traffic Control
The Contractor shall provide at its own cost for any necessary traffic control and access to the Works, and shall take all reasonable steps to ensure that its traffic and that of the Contractor's Personnel—
(1) complies with the restrictions concerning laden weight and dimensions in the Law and
(2) does not damage roads (except for ordinary wear) bridges or other property.

7.10 Condition of Site on Completion
As soon as practicable after the Works or any Section reaches Substantial Completion, the Contractor shall remove from the Site Contractor's Things not required to perform the Contractor's remaining obligations, and leave the Works or Section in an orderly manner. At the end of the Defects Period, the Contractor shall remove from the Site any remaining Contractor's Things. In this sub-clause 7.10, Contractor's Things includes temporary works that have not become part of the Works.

7.11 Working Times
The Contractor shall ensure that the Contractor's Personnel work on the Site only during the working times set out in the Works Requirements, if any, unless
(1) there is imminent danger to safety or health or of damage to the Works or other property or
(2) otherwise agreed with the Employer.

4.4 Clause 9 is amended as stated in the Works Requirements.

5. **Warranty**
The Specialist warrants to the Main Contractor that it has not breached any of its obligations under the Specialist Contract.

6. **Release from Obligations**

6.1 The Specialist will no longer owe any obligation to the Employer under the Specialist Contract. This does not affect any collateral warranty between the Specialist and the Employer.

6.2 Similarly, the Employer will no longer owe any obligation to the Specialist under the Specialist Contract.

7. **Law**
This Agreement is governed by and construed according to Irish law. The parties submit to the jurisdiction of the Irish courts in relation to all matters concerning it.

Given under the Specialist's common seal

Affix Specialist's common seal	
Signatures of persons authorised to authenticate the seal	

OR

Signed and delivered as a Deed by

Name of attorney	
Signature of attorney	
As lawful attorney of the Specialist under a power of attorney dated	

In the presence of

Name of witness	
Signature of witness	
Witness's occupation	
Witness's address	

OR

Signed on behalf of

Name of Specialist	
Signature of authorised person	

In the presence of

Name of witness	
Signature of witness	
Witness's occupation	
Witness's address	

OR (if the Specialist is an individual)

Signed and delivered as a Deed by

Name of Specialist	
Signature of Specialist	

In the presence of

Signature of witness	
Name of witness	
Witness's occupation	
Witness's address	

OR

Signed by

Name of Specialist	
Signature of Specialist	

In the presence of

Signature of witness	
Name of witness	
Witness's occupation	
Witness's address	

Given under the Main Contractor's common seal

Affix Main Contractor's common seal	
Signatures of persons authorised to authenticate the seal	

OR

Signed and delivered as a Deed by

Name of attorney	
Signature of attorney	
As lawful attorney of the Main Contractor under a power of attorney dated	

In the presence of

Name of witness	
Signature of witness	
Witness's occupation	

Witness's address	

OR
Signed on behalf of

Name of Main Contractor	
Signature of authorised person	

In the presence of

Name of witness	
Signature of witness	
Witness's occupation	
Witness's address	

OR (if the Main Contractor is an individual)
Signed and delivered as a Deed by

Name of Main Contractor	
Signature of Main Contractor	

In the presence of

Signature of witness	
Name of witness	
Witness's occupation	
Witness's address	

OR
Signed by

Name of Main Contractor	
Signature of Main Contractor	

In the presence of

Signature of witness	
Name of witness	
Witness's occupation	

Witness's address	

OR (if the Main Contractor is a joint venture, execution must be by each member, using the blocks below)

Joint Venture Member 1

Given under the common seal of

Name of joint venture member 1	
Affix common seal	
Signatures of persons authorised to authenticate the seal	

OR

Signed and delivered as a Deed by

Name of attorney	
Signature of attorney	
As lawful attorney of joint venture member 1 under a power of attorney dated	

In the presence of

Name of witness	
Signature of witness	
Witness's occupation	
Witness's address	

OR

Signed on behalf of

Name of joint venture member 1	
Signature of authorised person	

In the presence of

Name of witness	
Signature of witness	
Witness's occupation	
Witness's address	

Joint Venture Member 2

Given under the common seal of

Name of joint venture member 2	
Affix common seal	
Signatures of persons authorised to authenticate the seal	

OR

Signed and delivered as a Deed by

Name of attorney	
Signature of attorney	
As lawful attorney of joint venture member 2 under a power of attorney dated	

In the presence of

Name of witness	
Signature of witness	
Witness's occupation	
Witness's address	

OR

Signed on behalf of

Name of joint venture member 2	
Signature of authorised person	

In the presence of

Name of witness	
Signature of witness	
Witness's occupation	
Witness's address	

Joint Venture Member 3

Given under the common seal of

Name of joint venture member 3	
Affix common seal	
Signatures of persons authorised to authenticate the seal	

OR

Signed and delivered as a Deed by

Name of attorney	
Signature of attorney	

As lawful attorney of joint venture member 3 under a power of attorney dated	

In the presence of

Name of witness	
Signature of witness	
Witness's occupation	
Witness's address	

OR

Signed on behalf of

Name of joint venture member 3	
Signature of authorised person	

In the presence of

Name of witness	
Signature of witness	
Witness's occupation	
Witness's address	

Given under the Employer's seal

Affix Employer's seal	
Signatures of persons authorised to authenticate the seal	

OR

Signed on behalf of the Employer

Signature of authorised person	

In the presence of

Name of witness	

Signature of witness	
Witness's occupation	
Witness's address	

Note
Novation is where the Contractor takes over the role and responsibilities of the Employer in relation to a contract that the Employer has with another party. This arises where an Employer enters into a contract with another party with the intention that at some time during that contract the main Contractor will replace the Employer through a novation arrangement. MF 1.9 is the model of the novation agreement that may be used in all other circumstances except where the contract is being novated to a Joint Venture.

MODEL FORM 1.10

Appointment of Project Supervisor[1]

THIS AGREEMENT is made on [ ] **BETWEEN**

1. *The **Client*** [ ]

Whose principal office is at [ ]

and

2. *The **Project Supervisor*** [ ]

Whose registered office is at [ ]

BACKGROUND

A. By a contract (the **Contract**) made on or about [ ][2], the Client, as employer, has appointed [ ][3] as contractor (the **Contractor**) for

Name of Contract [ ]

(the **Works**).

B. This Agreement is collateral to the Contract.

C. Terms defined in the Contract have the same meaning in this Agreement. The terms **competent person** and **relevant statutory provisions** are construed according to section 2 of the Safety, Health and Welfare at Work Act 2005 and any amendment to it.

IT IS AGREED AS FOLLOWS:

1. The Client appoints the Project Supervisor as project supervisor for the construction stage according to the Safety, Health and Welfare (Construction) Regulations 2013 and any amendment to them (the **Construction Regulations**) for the project comprising

the Works

[and][4]

(the **Project**).

2. The Project Supervisor's appointment starts on the date of this Agreement and continues for as long as, under the Construction Regulations, the Client is required to have a project supervisor for the construction stage for the Project, unless the appointment is terminated earlier.

3. The Project Supervisor accepts the appointment.

4. The Project Supervisor shall perform all of its duties under the Construction Regulations as project supervisor for the construction stage for the Project.

5. The Project Supervisor represents and warrants to the Client that the Project Supervisor is and will continue to be a competent person to carry out its duties under this Agreement and the Construction Regulations and has allocated and will allocate sufficient resources to enable itself to comply with the requirements and prohibitions imposed on the Project Supervisor by this Agreement and under the relevant statutory provisions. In this Agreement, **competent person** and **relevant statutory provisions** are construed according to section 2 of the Safety, Health and Welfare at Work Act 2005 and any amendment to it.

---

[1] If the Project Supervisor is not incorporated in Ireland, execution will be in accordance with the law of its jurisdiction of incorporation for execution in Ireland

[2] Date of letter of acceptance

[3] Insert "the Project Supervisor" or the name of the Contractor, as appropriate.

[4] Specify any additional scope for which this Project Supervisor is to be appointed – for example, a process installation.

6. The Project Supervisor represents and warrants to the Client that the time allowed by the Contract for the completion of the Works is appropriate and sufficient to enable the Project Supervisor to perform its duties under this Agreement and the Construction Regulations.

7. The Project Supervisor represents and warrants to the Client that the information provided by the Client to the Project Supervisor about the state or condition of the Site (as defined in the Contract) and any premises on it is appropriate and sufficient to enable the Project Supervisor to perform its duties under this Agreement and the Construction Regulations.

8. The Project Supervisor shall ensure that it is insured by insurances in the same terms as the insurances the Contractor is required to have under clauses 3.6 and 3.7 of the Conditions of the Contract, and that those insurances comply with all the requirements of the Contract, and are kept in force for the same period as required by the Contract, and include cover for death or injury resulting from the Project Supervisor's performance or non-performance of its duties under this Agreement and the Construction Regulations.

9. Payment for the Project Supervisor's service is provided for under the Contract. Accordingly, the Client is not liable under this Agreement for the Project Supervisor's fees or expenses.

10. If the Project Supervisor breaches its obligations or warranties under this Agreement, or if the Contractor's duty to complete the Works is terminated under the Contract, the Client may terminate the Project Supervisor's appointment under this Agreement.

11. Without limiting its obligations under the Construction Regulations, the Project Supervisor shall give the Client all documents it prepares in the course of and for the purpose of performing its duties under this Agreement (**Project Supervisor's Documents**). If the Project Supervisor's appointment under this Agreement terminates, the Project Supervisor shall give all Project Supervisor's Documents to the Client immediately. Ownership of and copyright in the Project Supervisor's Documents shall become the Client's when the Project Supervisor delivers them to the Client, or the appointment is terminated, whichever is earlier. The Project Supervisor shall indemnify the Client against any liability resulting from the use or copying of the Project Supervisor's Documents infringing the property (including intellectual property) rights of any person.

12. This Agreement is governed by and construed according to Irish law. The parties submit to the jurisdiction of the Irish courts in relation to all matters concerning it.

Given under the Client's seal

Affix Client's seal	
Signatures of persons authorised to authenticate the seal	

OR

Signed on behalf of the Client

Signature of authorised person	

In the presence of

Name of witness	
Signature of witness	
Witness's occupation	
Witness's address	

Given under the Project Supervisor's common seal

Affix Project Supervisor's common seal	
Signatures of persons authorised to authenticate the seal	

OR

Signed, sealed and delivered by

Name of attorney	
Signature of attorney	
As lawful attorney of the Project Supervisor under a power of attorney dated	
Affix attorney's personal seal	

In the presence of

Name of witness	
Signature of witness	
Witness's occupation	
Witness's address	

OR

Signed on behalf of

Name of the Project Supervisor	
Signature of authorised person	

In the presence of

Name of witness	
Signature of witness	
Witness's occupation	
Witness's address	

OR (if the Project Supervisor is an individual)

Signed, sealed and delivered by

Name of Project Supervisor	
Signature of Project Supervisor	
Affix personal seal	

In the presence of

Signature of witness	
Name of witness	
Witness's occupation	
Witness's address	

OR

Signed by

Name of Project Supervisor	
Signature of Project Supervisor	

In the presence of

Name of witness	
Signature of witness	
Witness's occupation	
Witness's address	

Note

This is a model of the form to be used when the Contractor is appointed as Project Supervisor for the Construction Stage (PSCS) or as Project Supervisor for the Design Process (PSDP) and PSCS. It is also used when a Contractor's nominee is appointed as PSDP.

MODEL FORM 1.11

Professional Indemnity Insurance Certificate

(Clause 3.9.6)

To:	*The **Employer***	
	Address of Employer	
Date:		

Regarding:	*The Contract*	
	Name of Contractor	

From:	*Name of Broker/ Underwriter*	
	Address of Broker/ Underwriter	

A Dhaoine Uaisle

We are the insurance brokers/underwriter in relation to the Contractor's professional indemnity insurance. We confirm that the details of the Contractor's professional indemnity insurance set out below are true and accurate in all respects.

Name of Insurance Company		
Address of Insurance Company		
Policy No.(s)		
Retroactive Date(s)		
Renewal Date(s)		
Occupation as stated in the policy(ies)		
Limit of Indemnity	Any One Claim	€
	Any One Period	€
Amount of Policy Excess, if any		€
Territorial Limits in relation to the insurance		
Jurisdiction is limited to		

The insurance includes legal liability in respect of	death, bodily injury or disease to persons (other than employees) resulting from breach of the Contractor's professional duties	Yes
	damage to third party property resulting from breach of the Contractor's professional duties	Yes
The insurance covers claims arising out of the sub-contracting of design or supervision activities, if any, to sub-contractors		Yes
The adequacy of the professional indemnity insurances arranged by such sub-contractors has been investigated and confirmed		Yes
The insurance includes	Liability as project supervisor for design process	Yes
	Liability as project supervisor for construction stage	Yes
	Liability under Collateral Warranties or Duty of Care Agreements	Yes
The insurance provides full policy cover in respect of	Date Recognition / Year 2000 problems	Yes
	Pollution / contamination	Yes
	Composite panels	Yes
	Asbestos	Yes

Is mise, le meas

Signed

____

On behalf of the Insurer or Insurance Broker

Note
This is a model of the form used to certify that the Contractor has professional indemnity insurance. Where it is requested, the Contractor is responsible for maintaining professional indemnity insurance in relation to design negligence. It may be required on traditional contracts where there is a large amount of Contractor or Specialist design, and it is always required on all contractor-designed projects.

MODEL FORM 1.12

Collateral Warranty[1]

(Clause 5.5)

THIS DEED is made on [ ] **BETWEEN:**

1. *The **Specialist*** [ ]

Registered office of Specialist [ ]

2. *The **Contractor*** [ ]

Registered office of Contractor [ ]

and

3. *The **Employer*** [ ]

Whose principal office is at [ ]

BACKGROUND

A. The Employer has entered or is about to enter into a contract with the Contractor for

Name of Contract [ ]

(the **Works**)

on behalf of the Employer.

B. Terms defined in the Contract have the same meaning in this Deed.

C. By written agreement dated [ ] (the **Contract**) the Contractor has appointed the Specialist to

Description of contract works or services or supply [ ]

in connection with the Works.

D. The total amount to be paid by the Contractor to the Specialist under the Contract for completing the Specialist's obligations under the Contract is € [ ].

IT IS AGREED as follows in consideration of the payment of €1 by the Employer to the Specialist (receipt of which the Specialist acknowledges):

1. Specialist's Undertakings to the Employer

1.1 The Specialist warrants and undertakes to the Employer that it has not broken and will not break any express or implied term of the Contract.

1.2a[2] The Specialist covenants with the Employer that, in carrying out the Contract, the Specialist has exercised and will continue to exercise the standard of skill, care and diligence reasonably to be expected of properly qualified persons providing works, services or supply comparable in value, size, scope, complexity and quality to that required under the Contract.

---

[1] If the Specialist and/or the Contractor is/are not incorporated in Ireland, execution will be in accordance with the law of its jurisdiction of incorporation for execution in Ireland.

[2] 1.2a and 1.2b are alternatives: if 1.2b applies it means that the Specialist is not a consultant and therefore text in 1.2a should be deleted and the words "(sub-clause not used)" inserted.

1.2b[3] The Specialist covenants with the Employer that, in carrying out the Contract, the part of the Works to be undertaken by the Specialist, when complete, will be fit for its intended purpose as described in the Contract.

2. Insurance

2.1a[4] The Specialist shall maintain professional indemnity insurance in the amount of at least € covering the Specialist's obligations under this Deed for each and every claim or series of claims arising from the same originating cause until a date no earlier than six years from the date of Substantial Completion of the Works is certified under the Contract.

2.1b[5] The Specialist shall maintain professional indemnity insurance in the amount of at least € on an annual aggregate limit until a date no earlier than six years from the date of Substantial Completion of the Works is certified under the Contract.

2.2 The maximum excess shall be € .

2.3 When it is reasonably requested to do so by the Employer, the Specialist shall produce for inspection satisfactory documentary evidence that its professional indemnity insurance is being maintained.

2.4 The Specialist shall immediately notify the Employer of any cancellation, non-renewal or material reduction in the insurance.

3. Copyright

3.1[6] Ownership of and copyright in all Contractor's Documents provided or produced by or on behalf of the Specialist will transfer to the Employer when the Employer receives them.

3.2 The copyright in all drawings, designs, reports, specifications, calculations and other similar documents and written information (including all information stored on any disk, computer or processing facility) obtained or provided by or on behalf of the Specialist in connection with the Works, other than Contractors Documents[7] (**Design Information**) will remain vested in the Specialist.

3.3 The Specialist grants to the Employer, and all those authorised by it, an irrevocable royalty free non-exclusive licence to copy and use Design Information and to reproduce the designs contained in them for any purpose related to the Works including, but without limitation, to construct, complete, maintain, extend, let, sell, promote, advertise, reinstate and repair the Works.

3.4 The Specialist will not be liable for any use by the Employer of the Contractor's Documents or Design Information for any purpose other than that for which the Specialist prepared and provided them.

3.5 The Specialist shall pay and indemnify the Employer against all royalties and other sums for the supply and use of any patented or copyrighted articles, processes, information or investigations required to perform its duties under the Contract.

3.6 The Specialist shall, on reasonable demand, produce to the Employer a copy of all the Contractor's Documents and Design Information.

3.7 The Specialist shall indemnify the Employer against losses, liability, damages, claims, proceedings and costs suffered or incurred by reason of the Specialist infringing or being held to have infringed any copyright or other intellectual property rights in any Contractor's Documents or Design Information.

4. Assignment

The benefit of this Deed is assignable.

5. Step In

5.1 The Employer has no authority under this Deed to issue any instruction to the Specialist in relation to the Specialist's duties under the Contract, unless and until the Employer has given notice under sub-clause 5.3 below.

---

[3] 1.2a and 1.2b are alternatives: if 1.2a applies the text in 1.2b should be deleted and the words "(sub-clause not used)" inserted. If both sub-clauses 1.2a and 1.2b are left in or deleted the default text for the sub-clause is "The Specialist covenants with the Employer that, in carrying out the Contract, the part of the Works to be undertaken by the Specialist, when complete, will be fit for its intended purpose as described in the Contract."

[4] 2.1a and 2.1b are alternatives: if 2.1b applies it means that the Specialist is not a consultant and therefore the text in 2.1a should be deleted and the words "(sub-clause not used)" inserted.

[5] 2.1a and 2.1b are alternatives: If 2.1a applies the text in 2.1b should be deleted and the words "(sub-clause not used)" inserted. If both sub-clauses 2.1a and 2.1b are left in or deleted the default text for the sub-clause is "The Specialist shall maintain professional indemnity insurance in the amount of at least €6,500,000.00 on an annual aggregate limit until a date no earlier than six years from the date Substantial Completion of the Works is certified under the Contract."

[6] Include 3.1 only if required under the main contract (Schedule, part 1O); otherwise delete it and insert the words "(sub-clause not used)".

[7] The text 'other than Contractors Documents' should only be included if assignment of copyright is required.

5.2 The Specialist agrees that it will not, without first giving the Employer at least 28 days written notice, exercise any right of termination of the Contract, or treat the Contract as having been repudiated, or discontinue carrying out the Contract. The notice to the Employer must be accompanied by all of the information referred to in sub-clause 5.5 below. The Specialist's rights of termination (and the like) will cease if, within the 28 day period, the Employer gives notice to the Specialist under sub-clause 5.3 below.

5.3 The Specialist agrees that, if the Employer gives notice requiring the Specialist to accept the Employer's instructions to the exclusion of the Contractor, the Specialist will deal with and accept instructions solely from the Employer in substitution for the Contractor as if the Employer had appointed the Specialist originally on the terms of the Contract.

5.4 Only if the Employer gives notice under sub-clause 5.3 above, the Employer will become liable for payment of the amounts payable to the Specialist under the Contract (except for amounts due for work for which the Employer has already paid the Contractor) and for performance of the Contractor's other obligations under the Contract, but the Employer's liability will not exceed the amounts particulars of which were given in the notice under sub-clause 5.2 above.

5.5 The Specialist and the Contractor shall, if so required by the Employer at any time, give the Employer a copy of the whole Contract, particulars of the amounts paid to the Specialist under the Contract, particulars of amounts due and unpaid to the Specialist, particulars of amounts remaining to be paid to the Specialist under the Contract but not yet due, and any information requested by the Employer that is relevant to these amounts.

5.6 If the Contractor's obligation to complete the Works is terminated under the contract between the Employer and the Contractor for the Works, and the Employer so requires, the Specialist shall enter into a contract with the Employer or a replacement contractor for the Specialist to complete its obligations under the Contract, in the same terms as the Contract with all necessary changes.

5.7 The Contractor releases the Specialist from any obligation to inquire about whether the Employer's rights under this clause have become exercisable, and from any liability to the Contractor for complying with this clause.

6. Notices

Any notice to be given under this Deed must be in writing and will be considered given if delivered by hand or sent by prepaid registered post to the address of the relevant party at the top of this Deed, or at any other address the relevant party may specify by written notice to the other parties. A notice will be taken to have been received on the day of delivery if delivered by hand, or 48 hours later if sent by prepaid registered post.

7. Common Law Rights

Nothing in this Deed limits the Employer's rights at law.

8. Law

This Deed is governed by and construed according to Irish law. The parties submit to the jurisdiction of the Irish courts in relation to all matters concerning it.

9. Procedure

If there is a conflict between this Deed and the Contract, this Deed takes precedence.

10. Joint and Several Liability

The obligations in this Deed of the persons comprising the Specialist are joint and several.

Given under the Specialist's common seal

Affix Specialist's common seal	
Signatures of persons authorised to authenticate the seal	

OR

Signed, sealed and delivered by

Name of attorney	
Signature of attorney	
As lawful attorney of the Specialist under a power of attorney dated	
Affix attorney's personal seal	

In the presence of

Name of witness	
Signature of witness	
Witness's occupation	
Witness's address	

OR

Signed on behalf of

Name of Specialist	
Signature of authorised person	

In the presence of

Name of witness	
Signature of witness	
Witness's occupation	
Witness's address	

OR (if the Specialist is an individual)

Signed and delivered as a deed by

Name of Specialist	
Signature of Specialist	
Affix personal seal	

In the presence of

Signature of witness	
Name of witness	
Witness's occupation	
Witness's address	

OR

Signed by

Name of Specialist	
Signature of Specialist	

In the presence of

Signature of witness	
Name of witness	
Witness's occupation	
Witness's address	

Given under the Contractor's common seal

Affix Contractor's common seal	
Signatures of persons authorised to authenticate the seal	

OR

Signed, sealed and delivered by

Name of attorney	
Signature of attorney	
As lawful attorney of the Contractor under a power of attorney dated	
Affix attorney's personal seal	

In the presence of

Name of witness	
Signature of witness	
Witness's occupation	
Witness's address	

OR

Signed on behalf of

Name of Contractor	
Signature of authorised person	

In the presence of

Name of witness	
Signature of witness	
Witness's occupation	
Witness's address	

OR (if the Contractor is an individual)

Signed and delivered as a deed by

Name of Contractor	
Signature of Contractor	
Affix personal seal	

In the presence of

Signature of witness	
Name of witness	
Witness's occupation	
Witness's address	

OR

Signed by

Name of Contractor	
Signature of Contractor	

In the presence of

Signature of witness	
Name of witness	
Witness's occupation	
Witness's address	

OR (if the Contractor is a joint venture, execution must be by each member, using the blocks below)

Joint Venture Member 1

Given under the common seal of

Name of joint venture member 1	
Affix common seal	
Signatures of persons authorised to authenticate the seal	

OR

Signed, sealed and delivered by

Name of attorney	
Signature of attorney	
As lawful attorney of joint venture member 1 under a power of attorney dated	
Affix attorney's personal seal	

In the presence of

Name of witness	
Signature of witness	
Witness's occupation	
Witness's address	

OR

Signed on behalf of

Name of joint venture member 1	
Signature of authorised person	

In the presence of

Name of witness	
Signature of witness	
Witness's occupation	
Witness's address	

Joint Venture Member 2

Given under the common seal of

Name of joint venture member 2	
Affix common seal	
Signatures of persons authorised to authenticate the seal	

OR

Signed, sealed and delivered by

Name of attorney	
Signature of attorney	
As lawful attorney of joint venture member 2 under a power of attorney dated	
Affix attorney's personal seal	

In the presence of

Name of witness	
Signature of witness	
Witness's occupation	
Witness's address	

OR

Signed on behalf of

Name of joint venture member 2	
Signature of authorised person	

In the presence of

Name of witness	
Signature of witness	
Witness's occupation	
Witness's address	

Joint Venture Member 3

Given under the common seal of

Name of joint venture member 3	
Affix common seal	
Signatures of persons authorised to authenticate the seal	

OR

Signed, sealed and delivered by

Name of attorney	
Signature of attorney	
As lawful attorney of joint venture member 3 under a power of attorney dated	
Affix attorney's personal seal	

In the presence of

Name of witness	
Signature of witness	
Witness's occupation	
Witness's address	

OR

Signed on behalf of

Name of joint venture member 3	
Signature of authorised person	

In the presence of

Name of witness	
Signature of witness	
Witness's occupation	
Witness's address	

Given under the Employer's seal

Affix Employer's seal	
Signatures of persons authorised to authenticate the seal	

OR

Signed on behalf of the Employer

Signature of person authorised to sign contracts on behalf of the Employer	

In the presence of

Name of witness	
Signature of witness	
Witness's occupation	
Witness's address	

Note

This is the model of the form of collateral warranty used to create a contractual link between specialists and the Employer. A collateral warranty is a form of deed that seeks to create a contractual link between the Employer and specialists contracted to the main works contractor. This can be of value where, for example, the main works contractor becomes bankrupt, as the Employer has step-in rights by virtue of the collateral warranty, and the Employer also has access to the specialists in relation to their design liability.

MODEL FORM 1.13

Rates of Pay and Conditions of Employment Certificate

To:	*The Employer*	
	Address of Employer	
	For the attention of	
Date:		

From:	*The Contractor's Representative*	

Regarding:	*The Contract*		
	Period of interim statement	From	To

A Dhaoine Uaisle

We refer to the above Contract.

Terms defined in the Conditions of the Contract have the same meaning in this certificate.

The Contractor certifies that, in respect of the work to which the interim statement referred to above relates, clause 5.3 of the Contract has been observed by the Contractor and the employers of all work persons on the Site. This certification includes, but is not limited to, the following:

- the rates of pay and the conditions of employment (including in relation to pension contributions) of each work person comply with all applicable statutory provisions, and those rates and conditions have been no less favourable than those for the relevant category of work person in any employment agreements registered under the Industrial Relations Acts 1946 to 2004
- all wages and other money due to each work person have been paid in accordance with the Payment of Wages Act 1991 and have not been more than 1 month in arrears or unpaid
- payments due to be paid on behalf of each work person (including pension contributions, where applicable) have been paid
- all pension contributions and other amounts due to be paid on behalf of each work person, have been paid
- all deductions from payments to work persons required by law have been made and paid on, as required by Law
- in relation to the employment of work persons on the Site, the Safety, Health and Welfare at Work Act, 2005 and all employment law including the Employment Equality Act 1998, the Industrial Relations Acts 1946 to 2004, the National Minimum Wage Act 2000, regulations, codes of practices, legally binding determinations of the Labour Court and registered employment agreements under those Laws have been observed.

Is mise, le meas

Signed by

Name of Contractor	
Signature of Contractor i.e Contractor's Representative	

Note

This is a model of the certificate used to certify that the Contractor is compliant with the Industrial Relations Acts 1946 to 2004 and all other relevant legislative requirements.

MODEL FORM 1.14

Bond – Unfixed Works Items[1]

(Clause 11.2)

Bond No. ______________ BOND AMOUNT: €

THIS BOND (the Bond) is made on

BETWEEN

1.	*The Contractor*	
	Registered office of Contractor	
2.	*The Surety*	
	Registered office of Surety	

and

3.	*The Employer*	
	Principal office of Employer	

BACKGROUND

A. The Contractor has been appointed by the Employer for

Name of Contract ______________

(the Contract).

B. The Contractor has agreed to furnish this bond to the Employer as a condition of payment for certain offsite Works Items.

C. Terms defined in the Contract have the same meaning in this Bond.

IT IS AGREED AS FOLLOWS:

1. The Surety guarantees to the Employer that if the Contractor breaches the Contract or the Contractor's obligation to complete the Works is terminated under clause 12.1 of the Conditions the Surety will, subject to this Bond, pay all amounts for which the Contractor is liable under or as damages for breach of the Contract, as established under the Contract, taking into account all sums due to the Contractor under the Contract.

2. The liability of the Surety under this Bond will not exceed € ______________.
When the Employer's Representative notifies the Employer

2.1 that any of the off-site Works Items referred to in recital B above have been delivered to the Site and all of the requirements of clause 11.2(1) of the Conditions have been met in regard to them and

2.2 the amount that the Contractor would be entitled to be paid when the Works Items have been delivered to the Site and all the requirements of clause 11.2(1) of the Conditions met

the Surety's maximum liability will be reduced by the amount so notified.

3. No alteration in the Contract or in the extent or nature of the Works, and no allowance of time under the Contract, and no forbearance or forgiveness concerning the Contract by the Employer, will in any way release the Surety from liability under this Bond.

[1] If the Contractor and/or Surety is/are not incorporated in Ireland, execution will be in accordance with the law of its jurisdiction of incorporation for execution in Ireland.

4. The Surety will be released from its liability under this Bond on certification of Substantial Completion of the Works, except in relation to any breach by the Contractor or termination that has occurred before that date, written notice (including particulars of the breach or termination) of which the Employer has given the Surety within 4 weeks after this expiry date.

5. The Contractor undertakes to the Surety to perform its obligations under the Contract. This undertaking does not limit any rights or remedies of the Employer or the Surety.

6. The Contractor must promptly, and the Employer may, provide to the Surety by registered or hand-delivered letter to the Surety's registered office given above or to the agent named in clause 12 below a copy of any notice that the Contractor gives to or receives from the Employer under clause 12 of the Conditions. Breach by the Contractor of this obligation or failure to give notice will not give any defence to a call on this Bond.

7. The decision of a court or arbitrator in a dispute between the Employer and the Contractor will be binding on the Surety as to all matters concerning a breach of the Contract, termination under the Contract, and the Contractor's liability.

8. If the Surety is called on to pay the Employer's loss following a termination under clause 12.1 of the Conditions, the Surety may suggest a completion contractor to the Employer, but the Employer has no obligation to accept the suggestion.

9. The Surety will not be liable under this Bond for a breach or termination caused solely and directly by war, invasion, act of foreign enemies, hostilities (whether war is declared or not), civil war, rebellion, revolution or military or usurped power.

10. The Employer may assign the benefit of this Bond, without the Surety's or the Contractor's consent, by giving written notice to the Surety.

11. This Bond is governed by and construed according to Irish law and the parties submit to the jurisdiction of the Irish courts to determine all matters concerning it.

12. The Surety appoints

Name of Agent	
Address of Agent	

as its agent for service of legal proceedings. The Surety confirms that the named agent has been irrevocably appointed and the failure of the agent to notify the Surety of receipt of a document will not invalidate any proceedings or the service of the document.[2]

13. Money payable by the Surety under this Bond will be paid in euro in Ireland.

Given[3] under the Contractor's common seal

Affix Contractor's common seal	
Signatures of persons authorised to authenticate the seal	

[2] An address in Ireland is required when the Surety does not have a registered office in Ireland.

[3] If the Contractor and/or Surety is/are not incorporated in Ireland, execution will be in accordance with the law of its jurisdiction of incorporation for execution in Ireland.

OR

Signed, sealed and delivered by

Name of attorney	
Signature of attorney	
As lawful attorney of the Contractor under a power of attorney dated	
Affix attorney's personal seal	

In the presence of

Name of witness	
Signature of witness	
Witness's occupation	
Witness's address	

OR

Signed on behalf of

Name of Contractor	
Signature of authorised person	

In the presence of

Name of witness	
Signature of witness	
Witness's occupation	
Witness's address	

OR (if the Contractor is an individual)

Signed, sealed and delivered by

Name of Contractor	
Signature of Contractor	
Affix personal seal	

In the presence of

Signature of witness	
Name of witness	
Witness's occupation	
Witness's address	

OR

Signed by

Name of Contractor	
Signature of Contractor	

In the presence of

Signature of witness	
Name of witness	
Witness's occupation	
Witness's address	

OR (if the Contractor is a joint venture, execution must be by each member, using the blocks below)

Joint Venture Member 1

Given under the common seal of

Name of joint venture member 1	
Affix common seal	
Signatures of persons authorised to authenticate the seal	

OR

Signed, sealed and delivered by

Name of attorney	
Signature of attorney	
As lawful attorney of joint venture member 1 under a power of attorney dated	
Affix attorney's personal seal	

In the presence of

Name of witness	
Signature of witness	
Witness's occupation	
Witness's address	

OR

Signed on behalf of

Name of joint venture member 1	
Signature of authorised person	

In the presence of

Name of witness	
Signature of witness	
Witness's occupation	
Witness's address	

Joint Venture Member 2

Given under the common seal of

Name of joint venture member 2	
Affix common seal	
Signatures of persons authorised to authenticate the seal	

OR

Signed, sealed and delivered by

Name of attorney	
Signature of attorney	
As lawful attorney of joint venture member 2 under a power of attorney dated	
Affix attorney's personal seal	

In the presence of

Name of witness	
Signature of witness	
Witness's occupation	
Witness's address	

OR

Signed on behalf of

Name of joint venture member 2	
Signature of authorised person	

In the presence of

Name of witness	
Signature of witness	
Witness's occupation	
Witness's address	

Joint Venture Member 3

Given under the common seal of

Name of joint venture member 3	
Affix common seal	
Signatures of persons authorised to authenticate the seal	

OR

Signed, sealed and delivered by

Name of attorney	
Signature of attorney	
As lawful attorney of joint venture member 3 under a power of attorney dated	
Affix attorney's personal seal	

In the presence of

Name of witness	
Signature of witness	
Witness's occupation	
Witness's address	

OR

Signed on behalf of

Name of joint venture member 3	
Signature of authorised person	

In the presence of

Name of witness	
Signature of witness	
Witness's occupation	
Witness's address	

Given under the Surety's common seal

Affix Surety's common seal	
Signatures of persons authorised to authenticate the seal	

OR

Signed, sealed and delivered by

Name of attorney	
Signature of attorney	
As lawful attorney of the Surety under a power of attorney dated	
Affix attorney's personal seal	

In the presence of

Name of witness	
Signature of witness	
Witness's occupation	
Witness's address	

Note

This is the model of the form of bond that the Contractor must have in place as a condition of payment for certain unfixed or offsite works items. These are items that have not yet been incorporated into the works.

MODEL FORM 1.15

Retention Bond[1]

(Clause 11.3)

To:	*The Employer*		
	Address of Employer		
Date:			
Regarding:	*The Contract for*		
	Dated		(the **Contract**)
and	*The Contractor*		
	Address of Contractor		
From:	*The Surety*		
	Registered office of Surety		

In consideration of you making payment to the Contractor of sums that would otherwise be retained by you under the Contract, we (the Surety) undertake to pay to you (the Employer), without further proof or conditions and without deduction or set-off, any amount or amounts up to € ______ on receipt of your demand in writing.

Unless a demand has been made, our liability under this Bond will expire on ______[2].

Any demand must be in writing addressed to

______

and must be accompanied by your declaration that:

- the Contractor has failed to perform its obligations under the Contract or
- the Contractor's obligation to complete the Works has been terminated under the Contract or
- any of the events listed in clause 12.1 of the conditions of the Contract have happened

You may make one or more drawings under this Bond.

No alteration in the Contract or in the extent or nature of the works to be done under it, and no allowance of time under the Contract, and no forbearance or forgiveness concerning the Contract by the Employer, will in any way release us from liability under this Bond.

---

[1] If the Surety is not incorporated in Ireland, execution will be in accordance with the law of its jurisdiction of incorporation for execution in Ireland.

[2] Insert date 90 days after the end of the Defects Period.

We appoint

Name of Agent	
Address of Agent	

as our agent for the service of legal proceedings. We confirm that the named agent has been irrevocably appointed and the failure of the agent to notify us of receipt of a document will not invalidate any proceedings or the service of the document.[3]

This Bond is governed by and construed according to Irish law and the parties submit to the jurisdiction of the Irish courts to determine all matters concerning it.

Given[4] under our common seal

Affix common seal	
Signatures of persons authorised to authenticate the seal	

OR

Signed, sealed and delivered by

Name of attorney	
Signature of attorney	
As lawful attorney of the Surety under a power of attorney dated	
Affix attorney's personal seal	

In the presence of

Name of witness	
Signature of witness	
Witness's occupation	
Witness's address	

[3] An address in Ireland is required when the Surety does not have a registered office in Ireland.

[4] If the Surety is not incorporated in Ireland, execution will be in accordance with the law of its jurisdiction of incorporation for execution in Ireland.

Note
This is the model of the form of retention bond that the Contractor must give the Employer in return for payment that would otherwise be retained until the end of the Defects Period.

MODEL FORM 1.16

Appointment of Conciliator

(Clause 13 of PW-CF1 to PW-CF5 inclusive, Clause 15.2 of PW-CF6, Clause 10.8 of PW-CF10 and Clause 14.2 of PW-CF11.)

THIS AGREEMENT is made on [ ] **BETWEEN**

1.	*The Employer*	
	Principal office of Employer	
2.	*The Contractor*	
	Registered office of Contractor	

and

3.	*The Conciliator*	
	Address of Conciliator	

Whereas

A. The Employer and Contractor have entered into a contract dated [ ] (the **Contract**) for

Description of Works [ ]

B. The Contract provides for the appointment of a conciliator for the resolution of disputes referred to conciliation.

NOW IT IS HEREBY AGREED as follows:

1. The Conciliator shall act in accordance with the terms of the Contract.

2. For all purposes related to this agreement the Employer's, Contractor's and Conciliator's addresses are as follows:

2.1	*Employer's Address*	
2.2	*Contractor's Address*	
2.3	*Conciliator's Address*	

3. The Employer and the Contractor shall pay the Conciliator's fees and expenses as follows:[1]

where the conciliator to be appointed is the Standing Conciliator under the Contract, and the fees and expenses entered here differs from the fees and expenses at clause 7 under Model Form MF1.18 Appointment of Standing Conciliator, the fees and expenses entered here shall read as those from clause 7 under Model Form MF1.18 Appointment of Standing Conciliator

As between themselves, the Contractor and the Employer shall each pay one half of amounts due to the Conciliator under this agreement. As between the Conciliator and the other parties, the Employer and the Contractor are jointly and severally liable to the Conciliator. If one party pays the other's share of an amount due to the Conciliator, that party is entitled to reimbursement from the other.

4. This agreement remains in effect for as long as the Conciliator continues to act in that capacity.

5. This agreement is governed by and construed in accordance with Irish law.

6. Any dispute or claim arising out of or in connection with this agreement shall be settled by arbitration in accordance with the arbitration rules referred to in the Contract, amended as required.

Signed for and on behalf of the Employer

Signature of authorised person	

In the presence of

Name of witness	
Signature of witness	
Witness's occupation	
Witness's address	

Signed on behalf of[2]

Name of Contractor	
Signature of authorised person	

In the presence of

[1] Delete 'and expenses' if it does not apply; set out agreed terms or refer to separate letter.

[2] If the Contractor is not incorporated in Ireland, execution will be in accordance with the law of its jurisdiction of incorporation for execution in Ireland.

Name of witness	
Signature of witness	
Witness's occupation	
Witness's address	

OR (if the Contractor is an individual)

Signed by

Name of Contractor	
Signature of Contractor	

In the presence of

Signature of witness	
Name of witness	
Witness's occupation	
Witness's address	

OR (if the Contractor is a joint venture execution must be by each member, using the blocks below)

Joint Venture Member 1

Signed on behalf of

Name of joint venture member 1	
Signature of authorised person	

In the presence of

Name of witness	
Signature of witness	
Witness's occupation	
Witness's address	

Joint Venture Member 2

Signed on behalf of

Name of joint venture member 2	
Signature of authorised person	

In the presence of

Name of witness	
Signature of witness	
Witness's occupation	
Witness's address	

Joint Venture Member 3

Signed on behalf of

Name of joint venture member 3	
Signature of authorised person	

In the presence of

Name of witness	
Signature of witness	
Witness's occupation	
Witness's address	

Signed by the Conciliator

Signature of Conciliator	

In the presence of

Name of witness	
Signature of witness	
Witness's occupation	

Witness's address	

Note
This is the model form for appointing the conciliator who is engaged to assist in the resolution of any dispute between the Employer and the Contractor.

MODEL FORM 1.17

Bond – Conciliator's Recommendation

(Clause 13 of PW-CF1 to PW-CF5 inclusive)

To:	*The Beneficiary*	
	Address of Beneficiary	
Date:		

Regarding:	*The Contract for*		
	Dated		(the **Contract**)
between	*The Contractor*		
	Address of Contractor		
and	*The Employer*		
	Principal office of Employer		

From:	*The Surety*	
	Registered office of Surety	

A dispute has arisen under the Contract and the appointed conciliator has recommended that € ______ (the **Award Amount**) be paid to ______.

Clause 13.1.11, (Clause 13.2.11 of PW-CF1 to PW-CF4 inclusive of cited version 2.0 or later), of the conditions of the Contract provides that if a conciliator recommends payment of money, the party concerned must pay the amount recommended if the other party first provides a bond. This is that bond.

In consideration of your paying the Award Amount to ______ We, the Surety, undertake to pay to you, without further proof or conditions and without deduction or set-off, any amount or amounts up to the Award Amount on receipt of your demand in writing.

Unless a demand has been made, our liability under this Bond will expire on the earlier of:

- when you confirm to us in writing that the dispute that was the subject of the adjudication has been finally determined by an arbitrator or court, which has finally determined that ______ is entitled to the Award Amount net of any amounts owed to you.
- the date 550 days after the date of this Bond.

Any demand must be in writing addressed to ______
and either:

- be accompanied by your declaration that as a result of the award of an arbitrator or decision of a court, ______ is not entitled to the Award Amount net of any amounts owed to you or
- be made more than 500 days after the date of this Bond.

You may make one or more drawings under this Bond.

This Bond will become operative on payment by you of the Award Amount.

We will not be released in any way or discharged by time, indulgence, waiver, alteration, release or compromise or any other circumstances that might operate as a release of a guarantor at law or in equity.

This Bond is governed by and construed according to Irish law and the parties submit to the jurisdiction of the Irish courts to determine all matters concerning it.

We appoint

Name of Agent	
Address of Agent	

as our agent for the service of legal proceedings. We confirm that the named agent has been irrevocably appointed and the failure of the agent to notify us of receipt of a document will not invalidate any proceedings or the service of the document.[1]

Given[2] under our common seal

Affix common seal	
Signatures of persons authorised to authenticate the seal	

OR

Signed, sealed and delivered by

Name of attorney	
Signature of attorney	
As lawful attorney of the Surety under a power of attorney dated	
Affix attorney's personal seal	

In the presence of

Name of witness	
Signature of witness	
Witness's occupation	
Witness's address:	

[1] An address in Ireland is required when the Surety does not have a registered office in Ireland.

[2] If the Surety is not incorporated in Ireland, execution will be in accordance with the law of its jurisdiction of incorporation for execution in Ireland.

Note

If the conciliator recommends that the Employer should make a payment to the Contractor and the Employer does not agree with that recommendation, the Employer should issue a notice of dissatisfaction and make the payment subject to the receipt of a bond provided by the Contractor for the same amount as the payment. This form is a model for such a bond. The purpose of the bond is to cover the eventuality that the final resolution of the dispute (by arbitration) might reverse the conciliator's recommendation. This provision can also be utilised by the Contractor if the Contractor has to make a payment to the Employer on foot of a conciliators recommendation.

MODEL FORM 1.18

Appointment of Standing Conciliator

(Clause 13.2 of PW-CF1 to PW-CF4 inclusive (cited version 2.0 or later))

THIS AGREEMENT is made on [ ] **BETWEEN**

1.	*The Employer*	
	Principal office of Employer	
2.	*The Contractor*	
	Registered office of Contractor	

and

3.	*The Standing Conciliator*	
	Address of Standing Conciliator	

Whereas

A. The Employer and Contractor have entered into a contract dated [ ] (the **Contract**) for

Description of Works	

B. The Contract provides for the appointment of a Standing Conciliator in accordance with Schedule Part 1N of the Contract.

NOW IT IS HEREBY AGREED as follows:

1. The Parties shall appoint the Standing Conciliator in accordance with the Contract.
2. The Standing Conciliator accepts this appointment and undertakes to carry out the Standing Conciliator's duties in accordance with this Agreement and the terms of the Contract. The Standing Conciliator's duties are as appended to this Agreement.
3. For all purposes related to this Agreement the Employer's, Contractor's and Standing Conciliator's addresses are as follows:

3.1	*Employer's Address*	
3.2	*Contractor's Address*	
3.3	*Standing Conciliator's Address*	

TERM

4. The term of this Agreement ("Term") shall be:

> Start Date: *Starting Date of the Contract or the date of this Agreement*
>
> End Date: *The Date of Substantial Completion of the Contract*
>
> ***Term advisory note 1:*** *The Parties and the Standing Conciliator should set the dates above with due regard to the Contract duration.*
>
> ***Term advisory note 2:*** *The Parties and the Standing Conciliator may agree in writing to extend the term of this Agreement, on the same terms and conditions, where necessary.*

FEES

5. Subject to the provisions of this clause 5 the Employer and the Contractor shall pay the Standing Conciliator's Fixed Price Lump Sum fee, (Fees) in the manner set out in Appendix 2.

   a. Discharge of the Fees is subject to:

      i. Compliance by the Standing Conciliator with the provisions of this Agreement

      ii. The Standing Conciliator being in possession of a tax clearance certificate issued by the Revenue Commissioners

   b. Payment of the amount of Fees due (less any due deduction in withholding tax) shall be made within 30 days of the Standing Conciliator furnishing a valid invoice.

> *Fixed Price Lump Sum Fee: Insert Fixed Price Lump Sum Fee*
>
> ***Fees advisory note 1:*** *The agreed fee is for the performance of the duties of Standing Conciliator and shall be Fixed Price Lump Sum.*
>
> ***Fees advisory note 2:*** *Fees for conciliating a dispute, referred under Sub-clause 13.2, are not to be included in the Fixed Price Lump Sum fees for a Standing Conciliator. These are to be dealt under Clause 7 of this Agreement.*

6. As between themselves, the Contractor and the Employer shall each pay one half of amounts due to the Standing Conciliator under this Agreement. As between the Standing Conciliator and the Parties, the Employer and the Contractor are jointly and severally liable to the Standing Conciliator. If one Party pays the other's share of an amount due to the Standing Conciliator, that Party is entitled to reimbursement from the other Party.

APPOINTMENT AS CONCILIATOR

7. Under the Public Works Contract Forms PW-CF1 to PW-CF4 inclusive the Standing Conciliator shall act as conciliator for all disputes referred to conciliation under Sub-clause 13.2 of the Contract. The Parties shall pay the Standing Conciliator's fees and expenses[1] as conciliator for conciliating disputes referred to conciliation under Sub-clause 13.2 of the Contract as follows:

> *Insert fees and expenses for conciliator*
>
> ***Appointment as conciliator advisory note 1:*** *The agreed fees and expenses, (where required), above apply to the conciliation of disputes referred to conciliation under Sub-clause 13.2 of the Contract ("conciliator's fees").*

---

[1] Select the appropriate from the menu.

> ***Appointment as conciliator advisory note 2:*** *The conciliator's fees may be based on hourly rates and shall not form part of the Lump Sum Fixed Price fee under this Agreement, nor shall the conciliator's fees form part of the Contract Sum.*
>
> ***Appointment as conciliator advisory note 3:*** *The conciliator's fees shall be inserted in to Model Form MF1.16, Appointment of Conciliator.*

8. On his/her appointment as Standing Conciliator, the Parties shall provide the Standing Conciliator with a complete set of Contract Documents. During the term of this Agreement, the Parties shall furnish the Standing Conciliator with the following:

   a. any such amendments to the Contract Documents;
   b. all programmes as per Sub-clause 4.9 of the Contract, all Progress Reports as per Sub-clause 4.10 of the Contract and all minutes of meetings and objections thereto as per Sub-clause 4.16 of the Contract;
   c. any other correspondence agreed between the Parties to be circulated to the Standing Conciliator; and
   d. any other documents required by the Standing Conciliator in the performance of his/her duties, or required under the Contract to be issued to the Standing Conciliator.

9. The Standing Conciliator shall ensure his/her availability for all site visits, meetings, hearings as necessary to perform his/her duties.

10. The Standing Conciliator shall keep up to date with the Contract, the Works and the contractual relationship between the Parties.

11. The Standing Conciliator may, on his/her own initiative or at the request of either Party, but in either case with the agreement of both Parties, informally assist the Parties in resolving any disputes.

12. The Standing Conciliator may, with the agreement of both Parties, offer views, either orally or written, and in any case without prejudice, of the likely outcomes of a dispute under consideration.

13. The Standing Conciliator may, with the agreement of both Parties, hold separate meetings with each Party to the Contract.

TERMINATION

This Agreement shall terminate on expiry of the Term.

14. This Agreement shall terminate on expiry of the Term.

15. This Agreement may be terminated immediately:

   a. if the Standing Conciliator fails to act in accordance with this Agreement and any agreed duties appended to this Agreement;

   b. if the Standing Conciliator is unable for whatever reason to perform his/her obligations under this Agreement for a reasonable period of time;

   c. at any time at the joint election of the Parties.

16. The Standing Conciliator may terminate this Agreement on 60 days notice to the Parties.

17. When the Standing Conciliator ceases to be the Standing Conciliator following a termination under Clause 14, 15 or 16 of this Agreement he/she shall return to the Parties any unearned portion of any fee paid, or the Parties shall pay any outstanding amount due to the Standing Conciliator under this Agreement at the time the Standing Conciliator ceased to be the Standing Conciliator.

18. The Standing Conciliator shall return all confidential information under this Agreement within 60 days of termination.

CONFLICT OF INTEREST

19. The Standing Conciliator shall;

    a. have no interest, financial or otherwise in the Parties or the Contract except for payment under this Agreement or the Appointment of Conciliator Agreement;

    b. have not previously been employed as a consultant or otherwise by the Parties, except as disclosed in writing to the Parties before the signing of this Agreement.

CONFIDENTIALITY

20. The Standing Conciliator shall keep all details of the Contract, this Agreement and/or Standing Conciliator activities private and confidential and shall not publish or disclose any information pertaining to the Contract, this Agreement and/or Standing Conciliator activities without receipt of prior written consent from the Parties.

MISCELLEANOUS

21. The Standing Conciliator shall not assign, delegate or sub-contract any of his/her duties, without the agreement of the Parties to the Contract.

22. This Agreement is governed by and construed in accordance with Irish law.

23. Any dispute or claim arising out of or in connection with this Agreement shall be settled by arbitration in accordance with the arbitration rules referred to in the Contract, amended as required.

Signed for and on behalf of the Employer

Name of authorised person	
Signature of authorised person	

In the presence of

Name of witness	
Signature of witness	
Witness's occupation	
Witness's Address	

Signed on behalf of[2]

Name of Contractor	
Name of authorised person	

[2] If the Contractor is not incorporated in Ireland, execution will be in accordance with the law of its jurisdiction of incorporation for execution in Ireland.

Signature of authorised person	
In the presence of	
Name of witness	
Signature of witness	
Witness's occupation	
Witness's Address	

OR (if the Contractor is an individual)

Signed by

Name of Contractor	
Signature of Contractor	
In the presence of	
Name of witness	
Signature of witness	
Witness's occupation	
Witness's Address	

OR (if the Contractor is a joint venture execution must be by each member, using the blocks below)

Joint Venture Member 1

Signed on behalf of

Name of Joint Venture Member 1	
Signature of authorised person	
In the presence of	
Name of witness	
Signature of witness	
Witness's occupation	
Witness's Address	

Joint Venture Member 2

Signed on behalf of

Name of Joint Venture Member 2

Signature of authorised person

In the presence of

Name of witness

Signature of witness

Witness's occupation

Witness's Address

Joint Venture Member 3

Signed on behalf of

Name of Joint Venture Member 3

Signature of authorised person

In the presence of

Name of witness

Signature of witness

Witness's occupation

Witness's Address

Signed by the Standing Conciliator

Signature of Standing Conciliator

In the presence of

Name of witness

Signature of witness

Witness's occupation

Witness's Address

APPENDIX 1

DUTIES OF THE STANDING CONCILIATOR

Insert Duties of Standing Conciliator

Insert Duties of Standing Conciliator

Insert Duties of Standing Conciliator

Insert Duties of Standing Conciliator

Insert Duties of Standing Conciliator

Duties advisory note 1: *When completing this appendix The Parties and the Standing Conciliator should have due regard to the Contract and the Guidance Note GN 3.1.1, Dispute Resolution, of the Capital Works Management Framework available at http://constructionprocurement.gov.ie/.*

APPENDIX 2

AGREED PAYMENT TERMS FOR FEES OF THE STANDING CONCILIATOR

Insert terms of Payment of Fees to the Standing Conciliator

Payment Terms advisory note 1: *When completing this appendix The Parties and the Standing Conciliator should have due regard to the Duties of the Standing Conciliator as agreed and inserted in Appendix 1.*

MODEL FORM 1.19

Reserved Specialist Performance Bond[1]

(Clause 1(i)(1) of NN Sub Contract)

Bond No. [ ] BOND AMOUNT: € [ ]

THIS BOND is made on [ ] **BETWEEN**

1.	*The **NN Sub-Contractor***	
	Registered office of NN Sub-Contractor	
2.	*The **Surety***	
	Registered office of Surety	

and

3.	*The **Contractor***	
	Registered office of Contractor	

BACKGROUND

A. The Contractor and the NN Sub-Contractor have or will enter into a sub-contract for

Description of Works [ ]

(the **Sub-Contract**).

B. The NN Sub-Contractor has agreed to furnish a performance bond to the Contractor.

C. The conditions of contract governing the Sub-Contract are the Agreement and Conditions of Sub-Contract (NN) issued by the Construction Industry Federation (the Conditions)

D. Terms defined in the Sub-Contract have the same meaning in this Bond.

IT IS AGREED AS FOLLOWS:

1. If the NN Sub-Contractor's obligation to complete the Works is terminated under clause 12(a) of the Conditions the Surety will, subject to this Bond, pay the Contractor any amount for which the NN Sub-Contractor is liable under clause 12(b) of the Conditions.

2. If the NN Sub-Contractor breaches the Sub-Contract the Surety will, subject to this Bond, pay the Contractor any amount for which the NN Sub-Contractor is liable to the Contractor as damages for breach of the Sub-Contract, as established under the Sub-Contract, taking into account all sums due to the NN Sub-Contractor under the Sub-Contract.

---

[1] If the NN Sub-Contractor and/or Surety is/are not incorporated in Ireland, execution will be in accordance with the law of its jurisdiction of incorporation for execution in Ireland.

3. The liability of the Surety under this Bond will not exceed € . This amount will be reduced by half on issue of the Certificate of Substantial Completion of the Works under the contract between the Contractor and the Employer named under that contract, details of which have been supplied to the Surety.

4. No alteration in the Sub-Contract or in the extent or nature of the works to be done under it, and no allowance of time under the Sub-Contract, and no forbearance or forgiveness concerning the Sub-Contract by the Contractor, will in any way release the Surety from liability under this Bond.

5. The Surety will be released from its liability under this Bond 450 days[2] after the certificate of Substantial Completion of the Works has been issued under the contract between the Contractor and the Employer named under that contract, except in relation to any breach by the NN Sub-Contractor or termination that has occurred before that date, written notice (including particulars of the breach or termination) of which has been given to the Surety earlier than 4 weeks after this expiry date.

6. The NN Sub-Contractor undertakes to the Surety to perform its obligations under the Sub-Contract. This undertaking does not limit any rights or remedies of the Contractor or the Surety.

7. The Contractor may, but is not required to, provide to the Surety a copy of any notice that the Contractor gives to or receives from the NN Sub-Contractor under clause 12 of the Conditions.

8. The decision of a court or arbitrator in a dispute between the Contractor and the NN Sub-Contractor will be binding on the Surety as to all matters concerning a breach of the Sub-Contract, termination under the Sub-Contract, and the NN Sub-Contractor's liability.

9. If the Surety is called on to pay the Contractor's loss following a termination under clause 12(a) of the Conditions, the Surety may suggest a completion subcontractor to the Contractor, provided the proposed completion subcontractor is acceptable to the Contractor and meets the Contractor's obligations under the contract between the Contractor and the Employer named under that contract (details of which have been provided to the Surety).

10. The Surety will not be liable under this Bond for a breach or termination caused solely and directly by war, invasion, act of foreign enemies, hostilities (whether war is declared or not), terrorism, civil war, rebellion, revolution, or military or usurped power.

11. The Contractor may assign the benefit of this Bond, without the Surety's or the NN Sub-Contractor's consent, by giving written notice to the Surety.

12. This Bond is governed by and construed according to Irish law and the parties submit to the jurisdiction of the Irish courts to determine all matters concerning it.

13. Money payable by the Surety under this Bond will be paid in euro in Ireland.

14. The Surety appoints

Name of Agent:

Address of Agent:

---

[2] If not otherwise specified, read as 450 days.

[3] If the NN Sub-Contractor and/or Surety is/are not incorporated in Ireland, execution will be in accordance with the law of its jurisdiction of incorporation for execution in Ireland.

Given[3] under the NN Sub-Contractor's common seal

Affix NN Sub-Contractor's common seal	
Signatures of persons authorised to authenticate the seal	

as its agent for service of legal proceedings. The Surety confirms that the named agent has been irrevocably appointed and the failure of the agent to notify the Surety of receipt of a document will not invalidate any proceedings or the service of the document.[4]

OR

Signed, sealed and delivered by

Name of attorney	
Signature of attorney	
As lawful attorney of the NN Sub-Contractor under a power of attorney dated	
Affix attorney's personal seal	

In the presence of

Name of witness	
Signature of witness	
Witness's occupation	
Witness's address	

OR

Signed on behalf of

Name of NN Sub-Contractor	

4 An address in Ireland is required when the Surety does not have a registered office in Ireland.

Signature of authorised person	

In the presence of

Name of witness	
Signature of witness	
Witness's occupation	
Witness's address	

OR (if the NN Sub-Contractor is an individual)

Signed, sealed and delivered by

Name of NN Sub-Contractor	
Signature of NN Sub-Contractor	
Affix personal seal	

In the presence of

Signature of witness	
Name of witness	
Witness's occupation	
Witness's address	

OR

Signed by

Name of NN Sub-Contractor	
Signature of NN Sub-Contractor	

In the presence of

Name of witness	
Signature of witness	

Witness's occupation	
Witness's address	

OR (if the NN Subcontractor is a joint venture, execution must be by each member, using the blocks below)

Joint Venture Member 1

Given under the common seal of

Name of joint venture member 1	
Affix common seal	
Signatures of persons authorised to authenticate the seal	

OR

Signed, sealed and delivered by

Name of attorney	
Signature of attorney	
As lawful attorney of joint venture member 1 under a power of attorney dated	
Affix attorney's personal seal	

In the presence of

Name of witness	
Signature of witness	
Witness's occupation	
Witness's address	

OR

Signed on behalf of

Name of joint venture member 1	
Signature of authorised person	

In the presence of

Name of witness	

Signature of witness	
Witness's occupation	
Witness's address	

Joint Venture Member 2

Given under the common seal of

Name of joint venture member 2	
Affix common seal	
Signatures of persons authorised to authenticate the seal	

OR

Signed, sealed and delivered by

Name of attorney	
Signature of attorney	
As lawful attorney of joint venture member 2 under a power of attorney dated	
Affix attorney's personal seal	

In the presence of

Name of witness	
Signature of witness	
Witness's occupation	
Witness's address	

OR

Signed on behalf of

Name of joint venture member 2	
Signature of authorised person	

In the presence of

Name of witness	

Signature of witness	
Witness's occupation	
Witness's address	

Joint Venture Member 3

Given under the common seal of

Name of joint venture member 3	
Affix common seal	
Signatures of persons authorised to authenticate the seal	

OR

Signed, sealed and delivered by

Name of attorney	
Signature of attorney	
As lawful attorney of joint venture member 3 under a power of attorney dated	
Affix attorney's personal seal	

In the presence of

Name of witness	
Signature of witness	
Witness's occupation	
Witness's address	

OR

Signed on behalf of

Name of joint venture member 3	
Signature of authorised person	

In the presence of

Name of witness	

Signature of witness	
Witness's occupation	
Witness's address	

Given under the Surety's common seal

Affix Surety's common seal	
Signatures of persons authorised to authenticate the seal	

OR

Signed, sealed and delivered by

Name of attorney	
Signature of attorney	
As lawful attorney of the Surety under a power of attorney dated	
Affix attorney's personal seal	

In the presence of

Name of witness	
Signature of witness	
Witness's occupation	
Witness's address	

MODEL FORM 1.20

Notification to named Specialists of amounts included in Main Contract Payment Certificate for named Specialist works

(Clause 11.1.3)

Description of named Specialist works		
To:	*The **named Specialist***	
	Address of named Specialist	
Date:		

Regarding:	*The Main Contract*	Note to ER: The description of the main contract works set out in the Form of Tender and Schedule
	Main Contract Date	Note to ER: the date the Employer issued the Letter of Acceptance
	Main Contractor	Note to ER: Provide the name of the Main Contractor

From:	*Name of Employer's Representative*	

A Dhaoine Uaisle

I hereby inform you that in accordance with the terms of the Main Contract noted above, a certificate for payment dated (the Said Certificate) has been issued to the Main Contractor for presentation to the Employer.

The Main Contractor has been directed that in the Said Certificate the following amount has been included for works undertaken under the Sub-Contract covering the works described above.

Gross amount for the above named Specialist included in the Said Certificate	Gross amount for the above named Specialist included in the payment certificate immediately preceding the Said Certificate	Net amount for the above named Specialist included in the Said Certificate
€	€	€

All amounts are exclusive of VAT and before deduction of any retention percentages or amounts that the Employer or Main Contractor may be entitled to withhold on payments otherwise due under the Main Contract/Sub-Contract.

Is mise, le meas

____

Note to ER: Insert name, Employer's Representative.

SAMPLE LETTERS AND NOTICES

Letters and Notices for Contractors Using Public Works Contracts for Building and Civil Engineering Works Designed by the Employer

1. The Public Works Contracts for both Building and Civil Engineering Works designed by the Employer have a common factor – they require notification in writing by Contractors to the Employer and/or the Employer's Representative.
2. Such notifications may be formal notice expressed to be a condition precedent to the Contractor's rights under the Contract. In other cases notification in writing is necessary to ensure communication between the Contractor and the Employer's Representative and for the proper and more efficient operation of the Contract conditions.
3. Under traditional contracts many situations have been encountered where the lack of a formal written has been pleaded against Contractors (and Subcontractors). This can have the effect of barring them from remedies to which they would otherwise be entitled or of making it more difficult for them to secure their full contractual entitlements. The new Public Works Contracts places more emphasis on formalities, written notices and maintaining records.
4. The following set of Model Letters and Notices are prepared for consideration by Contractors.
5. Traditionally contractors have been anxious to preserve good relations between their clients and their clients' consultants; commercially, this is as important as observing contractual formalities. The new Public Works Contracts require formalities to be observed. When submitting letters and notices, Contractors are only carrying out what is required of them under the Contracts.
6. With the Public Works Contracts the importance of efficient project management and contract administration is of paramount importance. The requirement for contractors to adhere to procedural timetables as set down in the contract with regards to claims is now supported by the courts in other jurisdictions.

Condition 1.3.2 Inconsistency between Terms

If either party becomes aware of any inconsistency between terms of the Contract it shall promptly inform the other party.

TO THE EMPLOYER'S REPRESENTATIVE

We have discovered an inconsistency between ....(give relevant details).

We request your instruction under Condition 4.4 on this matter.

Yours etc.

Condition 1.5 Performance Bond

The Performance Bond must be provided to the Employer before the starting date. The starting date means the date the Contractor proposes to start executing the Works, as notified by the contractor to the Employer's Representative under sub-clause 9.1.

TO THE EMPLOYER

Re: Performance Bond

We enclose herewith the Performance Bond as required by Condition 1.5 of the Contract.

Yours etc

Cc Employer's Representative.

Condition 1.6 Parent Company Guarantee

If required, the Contractor must provide a copy of the parent company guarantee to the Employer.

TO THE EMPLOYER

Re: Parent company guarantee

We enclose herewith the parent company guarantee as required by Condition 1.6 of the contract.

Yours etc

Cc Employer's Representative.

Condition 3.9 General requirements concerning insurances,

3.9.6 – Within 10 working days of a request from the Employer, the Contractor must provide the Employer with evidence that insurances are in effect.

TO THE EMPLOYER

Re: Insurances

Pursuant to your request dated ....under Condition 3.9.6 of the Contract for Insurance Details we enclose herewith copies of the Contractor's Indemnity/ Public Liability and Employer's Liability/Professional Indemnity/Other (*delete as appropriate*) insurance certificates for your retention.

Yours etc

Cc Employer's Representative.

In addition the Employer shall be informed of any reduction, cancellation, renewal or non-renewal of the insurance.

Condition 4.2 Contractor's Representative and Supervisor

Details of the proposed Contractor's Representative and Supervisor must be supplied to the Employer's Representative

TO THE EMPLOYER'S REPRESENTATIVE

Re: Contractor's Representative and Supervisor

In accordance with Condition 4.2.3 of the Contract we enclose details of the Contractor's Representative/Supervisor for your records. The Contractor's Representative/Supervisor named in the Works Proposal is no longer available to us.

Yours etc

Condition 4.5 Instructions

4.5.2 – If the Employer's Representative gives an instruction and calls it a direction, but the contractor considers that it is a Change Order, the Contractor shall be entitled to give notice under sub-clause 10.3 and the issue determined under clause 10. In addition to the requirements of sub-clause 10.3, the Contractor must give this notice before starting to implement the instruction, otherwise it will be taken to be a direction.

TO THE EMPLOYER'S REPRESENTATIVE

Re: Employer's Representative Direction Number/reference xx

In accordance with sub-clause 4.5.2 of the Contract we give notice that we consider the above referenced Employer's Representative's direction to be a Change Order. We shall provide further details in accordance with sub-clause 10.3 in due course.

Yours etc

Condition 4.6

Works Proposals

4.6.2 – if any Works Proposals do not comply with the Contract or the initial Works Requirements or are physically impossible to comply with, the Contractor shall propose a change to the Works Proposals as necessary.

TO THE EMPLOYER'S REPRESENTATIVE

Re: Proposal for a Change to the Works Proposal

In accordance with Condition 4.6.2 of the Contract we propose the following change(s) to the Works Proposal:

Details

[Note: There shall be no extension of time or adjustment to the Contract Sum for this]

Condition 4.6.2 goes on to state: *If the Work Proposals need to be changed because of a change to the Works Requirements the Contractor shall propose a change. The contractor shall submit any change to the Works Proposals to the Employer's Representative.*

[This proposal comes under Item 1 of Section K of the Schedule and is a Delay Event and a Compensation Event].

Condition 4.7

Required Contractor Submissions

Unless the Works Requirements say that a different procedure is to apply, whenever the Contract requires that a document or proposed course of action be submitted to the Employer's representative, the following shall apply:

4.7.1 the Contractor shall give the document or a statement of the proposed action and all necessary supporting information to the Employer's Representative.

TO THE EMPLOYER'S REPRESENTATIVE

Re: Statement of Proposed Action

In accordance with Condition 4.7.1 of the Contract we submit the Statement of the proposed xxx Works together with all supporting information.

Yours etc

Note

- Employer Representative may object;
- Employer's Representative may request further information;
- Employer's Representative may object after he has enough information;
- Contractor shall make a new submission to meet any objection given within the period (4.7.8);
- Contractor may have to submit new submissions as necessary to perform his duties under the Contract and submit a programme showing his actual and current planned progress (4.7.9).

Condition 4.8 Value Engineering

The Contractor may provide the Employer's Representative with a value engineering proposal

TO THE EMPLOYER'S REPRESENTATIVE

Re: Value Engineering Proposal for [Details]

In accordance with Condition 4.8 of the Contract we enclose a Value Engineering Proposal for ....(details)

The proposal includes

(i) Proposed changes to the Contract
(ii) Proposed changes to the Contractor's Documents
(iii) Detailed breakdown of the original cost for the relevant Work
(iv) The projected cost of the proposal
(v) The proposed adjustment to the Contract Sum to reflect the saving.
(vi) The proposed changes to the programme.

Condition 4.9 Programme

Before the starting date the Contractor must submit a programme to the Employer's Representative

TO THE EMPLOYER'S REPRESENTATIVE

Re: Construction Programme

In accordance with Condition 4.9.1 of the Contract we enclose the construction programme for the works for your information.

Yours etc.

Condition 4.9 **Programme**

Before the starting date the Contractor must submit a programme to the Employer's Representative and the programme will identify dates when items are required from the Employer

TO THE EMPLOYER'S REPRESENTATIVE

Re: Dates of Information Required

i) Please supply all the reinforcement schedules for the project by ……..
ii) List all other items

Yours etc.

Condition 4.17 **Contractor's things not to be removed**

TO THE EMPLOYER'S REPRESENTATIVE

Re: Removal of Items from Site

In accordance with Condition 4.17 of the Contract we advise you that we intend removing the followings from site ……….. on ……...

Yours etc

Condition 5.4.1 **The contractor shall submit details to the Employer's Representative of any proposed specialist, other than one named in the Contract or when the Contract provides other procedures.**

TO THE EMPLOYER'S REPRESENTATIVE

Re: Proposed Specialists for the …….Works

In accordance with Condition 5.4.1 of the Contract we submit details of proposed specialist xxx Limited for the supply and installation of the xxx works.

Yours etc

Condition 5.4.5 **The Contractor shall not terminate, allow to be terminated or accept a repudiation of such a Contract without first submitting details to the Employer's Representative, except...**

TO THE EMPLOYER'S REPRESENTATIVE

In accordance with Condition 5.4.5 of the Contract we advise you of our intention to terminate the sub-contract with xxx Limited, the specialist appointed for the xxx works. The reason for the termination is ....

We propose to replace xxx Limited with xxx Limited.

Yours etc

Condition 7.8 **Archaeological Objects and Human Remains**

The contractor shall inform the Employer's Representative

TO THE EMPLOYER'S REPRESENTATIVE

Re: Archaeological Objects

In accordance with Condition 7.8 of the Contract we advise you of the discovery of .... on site. We have preserved the area concerned and await your instructions in this regard.

Yours etc.

Condition 8.3.3 **Inspection**

The Contractor shall notify the Employer's Representative before any work item that is to be inspected is covered or packed.

TO THE EMPLOYER'S REPRESENTATIVE

In accordance with Condition 8.3.3 of the Contract we advise you that ......Works/Items are available for your inspection. The ....Works/Items will be covered on ....date.

Yours etc.

Condition 9.1

Starting Date

TO THE EMPLOYER'S REPRESENTATIVE

Re: Starting Date

In accordance with Condition 9.1 of the Contract we advise you that we propose to commence works on ....(Date). This is the Starting Date under the Contract.

Yours etc

Requirements: i) Minimum 15 working days' notice to the Employer's Representative

ii) Maximum 20 working days after the Letter of Acceptance

Condition 9.2.3

Suspension

If a suspension that is not caused by a Contractor's breach lasts more than three months the Contractor may request the Employer's Representative permission to proceed

TO THE EMPLOYER'S REPRESENTATIVE

Re: Suspended Works

Further to your instruction dated .... reference ...... to suspend the Works, in accordance with Condition 9.2.3 we request permission to proceed with the Works.

Yours etc

Condition 9.2.3(2)

Suspension

If the Employer's Representative does not give permission within 28 days after being requested to do so, the Contractor may, by giving notice to the Employer's Representative, terminate the Contractor's obligations under the Contract. In addition a notice would have to be submitted under Condition 12.4.2 and sent to the Employer.

Condition 9.3.1

Delay and Extension of Time

If the Contractor becomes aware that the Works is being or is likely to be delayed it shall as soon as practicable notify the Employer's Representative of the delay and its cause.

TO THE EMPLOYER'S REPRESENTATIVE

Re: Notice of Delay (Number 1, 2, 3, etc. — a log of Delay Notices should be maintained)

We hereby give notice under Condition 9.3.1 of the Contract that we have today become aware that the Works are being delayed /or are likely to be delayed by reason of (state cause). We also advise that we shall provide full details of the delay and its effect on the programme within 40 days of this notice.

Yours etc.

Condition 9.6 Substantial Completion

The Contractor must request the Employer's Representative to certify Substantial Completion of the Works or part thereof.

TO THE EMPLOYER'S REPRESENTATIVE

Re: Request for Certificate of Substantial Completion

We hereby advise you that the Works (or section of the Works) will be substantially complete by .....(date). In accordance with Condition 9.6.2 of the Contract we request you to certify Substantial Completion on that date.

Yours etc.

Condition 10.3 Contractor's Claims

If the Contractor considers that there should be an extension of time or an adjustment to the Contract Sum he shall provide such notice to the Employer's Representative within 20 working days after becoming aware (or 20 working days from when he should have been aware) of something that would give rise to an entitlement. The notice must prominently state that it is being given under sub-clause 10.3.

TO THE EMPLOYER'S REPRESENTATIVE

Re: Notice of Contractor's Claim(s) issued under Sub-Clause 10.3 of the Contract (Date and Reference).

In accordance with Sub-Clause 10.3 of the Contract we hereby give you notice of our claim(s) for an Extension of Time/an Adjustment to the Contract Sum/any Other Entitlement Under or in Relation to the Contract (e.g. increased cost) (delete as applicable).

Yours etc

Within a further 20 working days the Contractor shall provide

TO THE EMPLOYER'S REPRESENTATIVE

Re: Contractor's Claim issued under Sub-Clause 10.3 of the Contract (Date and Reference)

Further to our Notice of Claim (Date and Reference) we enclose the following information in support of our claim:

i) Details of all relevant facts;
ii) A detailed calculation; and
iii) A proposal based on the calculation of the adjustment to be made to the Contract Sum;
iv) Details of the amount(s) of any other entitlement(s) claimed by the Contractor;
v) Details of the effect on programme and completion dates

Yours etc

Condition 11.1

Interim Payment

TO THE EMPLOYER'S REPRESENTATIVE

Re Interim Payment Statement Number (...)

In accordance with clause 11.1 we herewith submit our Statement for Interim Payment Number (...). We enclose the following details for your information:

- Statement showing the progress of the Works;
- The instalment that the Contractor should be paid;
- A detailed breakdown;
- Any supporting details the Employer's Representative requires;
- Certificate stating that the Contractor has complied in full with sub-clause 5.3 (Pay and Conditions of Employment).

Yours etc

Condition 12.3

Suspension by the Contractor

TO THE EMPLOYER

If the Employer fails to pay any amount due under clause 11, the Contractor may, on giving notice to the Employer, in accordance with the Construction Contracts Act 2013, suspend execution of the Works until the amount has been paid. On receiving the payment or notice has been served by either Party referring the dispute to Adjudication, the Contractor shall resume execution of the Works.

As a result of the Employer's failure to pay te amount due under Clause 11 in accordance with the Construction Contracts 2013, we hereby give notice of our intention to suspend the execution of the Works until the amount has being paid in full. This demand is issued in accordance with Sub-Clause 12.3 of the Contract.

Note
The administrative details for the issuing of such notices are contained in the Construction Contracts Act 2013, as found at: http://www.irishstatutebook.ie/eli/2013/act/34/enacted/en/html.

Condition 12.3 — Notice To Suspend Execution Of The Works

In accordance with Sub-Clause 11.1.3 of the Contract, the Employer's Representative issued payment certificate number [XXX] dated [XXX] certifying the amount of [€XXX] for payment.

In accordance with Sub-Clause 11.1.4 of the Contract, the Contractor raised invoice number [XXX] dated [XXX] for the amount of [€XXX]. A copy of the invoice was provided to the Employer on [DATE]. The due date for payment was [date employer received the invoice plus 21 days]

As a result of the Employer's failure to pay the amount of [€XXXX] by [DATE], the Contractor hereby gives notice, that should payment of the amount due remain unpaid for a further 7 days from the date of this notice, the Contractor hereby notifies its intention to suspend the execution of the Works. The suspension of the execution of the Works shall commence on [Date of notice plus at least 7 days].

This notice is issued in accordance with Sub-Clause 12.3 of the Contract and Section 5 of the Construction Contracts Act 2013.

Yours etc

Note
The administrative details for the issuing of such notices are contained in s 5 of the Construction Contracts Act 2013, as found at: http://www.irishstatutebook.ie/eli/2013/act/34/enacted/en/html.

The Contractor should comply with the stipulations of Sub-Clauses 4.14.2 (1) and 4.14.3 with regard to the service and receipt of the notice. In addition to Sub-Clause 12.3 notice, if suspension of the execution of the Works occurs, the Contractor should also serve notice under Sub-Clause 10.3 advising of the delay and report the event in accordance with Sub-Clause 4.10.2 (10).

Condition 13 — Disputes

TO THE EMPLOYER (REFER TO SECTION A, SCHEDULE, PART 1 FOR NAMES AND ADDRESSES)

We notify of a dispute under the Contract [details].

We advise you that this dispute is being referred to conciliation

This is given under sub-clause 13.1 of the Contract.

Yours etc

Note
The Contractor should comply with the stipulations of Sub-Clauses 4.14.2 (1) and 4.14.3 with regard to the service and receipt of the notice.

This notice is followed by a letter to comply with 13.1.2 for the agreement of a jointly appointed conciliator.

In the event of the parties failing to appoint a conciliator within 10 working days of the referral the conciliator shall be appointed by the appointing body or person named in the Schedule, Part 1N, on the application of either party.

Any dispute that can be referred to conciliation can be finally settled by arbitration provided the conciliator's recommendation is rejected by either party within the specified period.

INDEX